Becoming a
Genuine Leader

"Marilyn Mason's brilliant book *Becoming a Genuine Leader* will empower you. Starting by digging deeply into your life story and family history, she enables you to avoid derailing behaviors in order to flourish as your authentic self. I have learned a great deal from Marilyn, and so will you if you explore her wisdom and follow her counsel. You'll be very glad you did."
—Bill George, professor at Harvard Business School and
former chair and CEO of Medtronic

"Dysfunctional leaders are a dime a dozen and usually baffled by the source of their failure. The wisdom gained by Dr. Mason from decades of consultations with corporate managers shines through these pages. She takes you home again, to discover how you learned to negotiate in the first organization to which you belonged, your family. Her psychological insights are stunning. She illuminates the passage to authentic leadership."
—Gail Sheehy, author of *Passages* and *Understanding Men's Passages*

"The more we learn, the better we lead, and this is a resource for success in all you do."
—Jesse Fink, cofounder of Priceline.com, impact investor, and chairman of MissionPoint Capital Partners

"If you aspire to authentic leadership you need to read—and heed—this book."
—Alan M. Webber, cofounder of *Fast Company* magazine

"This is the rare, sanity-saving book on leadership we've all been waiting for—and the one that the world needs most."
—Harriet Lerner, Ph.D., author of *The Dance of Anger* and *Marriage Rules*

"Over a lifetime, Marilyn Mason has guided the great and small through the portals of personal discovery into wisdom and freedom. In this fascinating, readable book she describes a path to genuine leadership that is simple, but not easy. Investigate the shadows of the past, she says; go deep into exaltation and shame, find the hidden drivers in the buried stories, and then rise again to your full power!"
—Craig Barnes, lecturer, playwright, radio host, and author of award-winning books, including *In Search of the Lost Feminine* and *Democracy at the Crossroads,* and critically acclaimed plays, including *An Elizabethan Trilogy* and *A Nation Deceived*

Becoming a Genuine Leader

Succeed with Integrity by Exploring Your Past

Marilyn Mason, Ph.D.

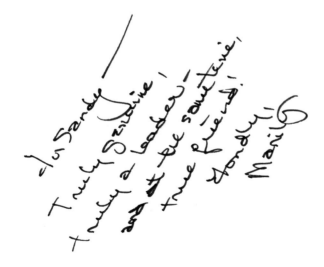

HAZELDEN®

Hazelden
Center City, Minnesota 55012
hazelden.org

© 2013 by Marilyn Mason, Ph.D.
All rights reserved. Published 2013.
Printed in the United States of America.

No part of this publication, either print or electronic, may be reproduced
in any form or by any means without the express written permission of
the publisher. Failure to comply with these terms may expose you
to legal action and damages for copyright infringement.

Library of Congress Cataloging-in-Publication Data

Mason, Marilyn.
    Becoming a genuine leader : succeed with integrity by exploring your
past / Marilyn Mason.
        pages cm
    Includes bibliographical references.
    ISBN 978-1-61649-477-3 (pbk.) — ISBN 978-1-61649-500-8 (epub)
    1. Leadership.   2. Leadership—Psychological aspects.   3. Interpersonal
relations.   4. Interpersonal communication.   I. Title.
    HD57.7.M39276 2013
    658.4'092—dc23

                                                                2013032982

Editor's note
The names, details, and circumstances may have been changed to protect the
privacy of those mentioned in this publication. In some cases, composites
have been created.
    This publication is not intended as a substitute for the advice of health care
professionals.
    Alcoholics Anonymous and AA are registered trademarks of Alcoholics
Anonymous World Services, Inc.

16 15 14 13   1 2 3 4 5 6

Cover design: David Spohn
Interior design: Kinne Design
Typesetting: BookMobile Design & Digital Publisher Services

To my committed family for accepting my ideas,
and to the many clients—individual and corporate—
who courageously faced their shadows of the
past to walk into the light of genuine leadership.

Contents

Acknowledgments

One of my editors once told me that publication is only an interruption in the life of a book. Oh, how true this is! This book has been traveling through many iterations—from *Family Ghosts in the Executive Suite* to *Invisible Loyalties at Work* to *Shadows in the Executive Suite*, and now, finally, *Becoming a Genuine Leader.* There are so many to acknowledge in my appreciation—my fear is that I am forgetting someone.

Since it is difficult to separate friends from colleagues (as so many are both), I shall combine the list of those who gave their loyal support throughout this process—a process that is a big part of my life. Many of the names listed are my personal board of directors with whom I can think out loud on almost any issue. Although they were not involved in this book's writing or editing, they have "had my back" throughout my life. They listened; they were all polite enough to not ask, "Marilyn, what is your book's title this week?" This list includes long-standing friends Constance Ahrons, Craig Barnes, Susan Boren, Ethelyn and Howard Cohen, Iris Cornelius, Carrell Dammann, Cece Derringer, Ruth Frazier, Jeannine Hall, Anna Hargreaves, Deborah Holloway, Helen Kornblum, Harriet Lerner, Constance and Michael Mierendorf, Joanie Shoemaker, Drew Stewart, and JoLynne Worley.

Going back to the early days, I must thank my coauthor, Merle Fossum, for our work together in *Facing Shame: Families in Recovery.* And Don Lamm, who gave the valuable feedback "Show us a way through." Special recognition goes to the work of Brené Brown, author of *Daring Greatly,* who took the shame concept to another level with her fine research on vulnerability.

Cathy Allen and Jeannine Hall have always been most generous in connecting me with the best of wisdom holders.

Alan Webber listened early on and shifted my thesis, reminding me that many pockets of excellent leadership exist beyond the boardroom!

Of course, my wonderful family was there from the beginning! Daughter Jeanine Stelli Esparolini and son-in-law Mark Esparolini, son Jerry Stelli and daughter-in-law Lorrie Warner, and my dear sister Sue Engelskirchen. I have so appreciated their candor throughout. They were most willing to hear concepts, send lists of possible titles (and title revisions), and most importantly, hear me.

And without the stories, what would this book be? Many thanks to Jesse and Betsy Fink, Bill George, Jeff George, Tony Gerlicz, Molly Kaufmann, Steve King, Mike Loftin, Rick Schnieders, Deborah Szekely, Alex von Bidder, and Alison Winter, and of course for the stories of Arie de Geus in his book *The Living Company*.

To the many executives and leaders who gave of themselves so generously but are not named here due to confidentiality (you know who you are!), without your stories, there would be no wisdom to pass on to others "on the path." Often people approach me and say, "Oh, I saw my story in your book," to which I would honestly have to reply, "Perhaps." Many of the stories here are composites of leaders I worked with along the way. I have changed settings, gender, and roles to protect these leaders and their families and firms. I must acknowledge some major influences in my professional development—Harry Levinson, Carl Whitaker, Huston Smith, and Virginia Satir. Although all but Huston are now deceased, I carry their teachings in my work.

Perhaps the greatest influential voice I followed in writing this book was that of Ivan Boszomenyi-Nagy, who, along with Geraldine Sparks, wrote the seminal work *Invisible Loyalties: Reciprocity in Intergenerational Family Therapy*, in which they focus on the invisible fabric of family loyalty.[1] In addition, Betty Carter and Monica McGoldrick added greatly to this concept.

And finally, special thanks to Sid Farrar and all the folks on the Hazelden team, a place dear to my heart.

· · · ·

Introduction

"Making sense of your past can change your future."

— DANIEL SIEGEL, M.D., AUTHOR OF *MINDSIGHT* AND
CODIRECTOR OF THE MINDFUL AWARENESS RESEARCH CENTER[1]

When I met Ted, I knew immediately that he did not want to be in my office; his board had just given him thirty days' notice to leave the large firm where he had been chief executive officer (CEO) for the past two years. As he sat tall, looking very distinguished in his finely finished dark woolen suit, I asked him where he thought he would like to start (we both knew the board chair had sent him to me for "exit consultation"). He crossed his arms and responded, in a most arrogant tone, "Well, I suppose you want me to sit here and talk mushy." Ted wore his false self like a coat of armor.

"Well," I replied slowly. "No, I would not say that—but talking honestly would do." It was clear that Ted did not have any personal agenda in mind; he did what the board requested—and no more! We both knew it was too late to save his present position; I reminded him it was not too late to save his personal and professional future. However, Ted chose not to do any self-reflection or evaluation of his past. A short time later, I learned that he had left the country to find another job that equaled his former position in the United States. After several of these exit interviews, I called my business consulting coach, Harry Levinson, a leading psychologist and management consultant from Harvard. I asked how it happened that so many board-fired CEOs had been hired in the first place. He quickly responded, in a matter-of-fact tone, "Well, they hired them for narcissism, domination, and control." This statement made total sense, supporting the daily reports we see in the media about greed-driven corruption in the business world. This hiring pattern has been in place for many decades; now we see the consequences.

Although realizing this meant I was no longer shocked in my consultations, I was troubled. What was driving the cultures of these firms? What were their leadership stories? Surely, a plethora of books, videos, and training programs addressed leadership, emotional intelligence quotient (EQ), personal development, and organizational cultures. What was missing? What was ignored? Evidently the multimillion-dollar, multinational business consulting firms were not faring well in this area either. In their book *The War for Talent*, three consultants at McKinsey & Company, one of the leading business consulting firms, describe a 1997 McKinsey study: when asked to name companies that excelled in rewarding the top leadership "talent," respondents praised Enron as "a company that thrives on . . . the chance to do something big."[2] Jeff Skilling, Enron CEO and former McKinsey employee, is now in his seventh year of a fourteen-year prison sentence for fraud.

Malcolm Gladwell later wrote a scathing article in *The New Yorker* disagreeing with the "talent war" approach of McKinsey, accusing those indulged "talent leaders" of being leaders who turned their responsibilities into huge losses.[3]

The good news, though, is that there is indeed a way through this complex tangle of interrelated issues, a path that can result in a win-win—personally for the potential "talent leader" and for the company culture as well. Sound too simple? In many ways, this path can be quite simple, but it is not easy. Taking this journey toward becoming what I call a "genuine leader" requires people to have the courage to look back and not only examine but also evaluate who they really are as leaders and how they grew into their leadership styles.

If you are reading this book, you most likely are in a leadership position or on a leadership track. Or perhaps you want to understand the leaders in your own organization. You too may wonder about the daily stories of exploitive, abusive, tyrannizing, and disappointing leadership. Perhaps you have felt confounded to search online for the phrase "genuine leadership" and find over *twenty-one million* results! Then you look around and wonder, "Who and where are the genuine leaders?" As you continue your search for answers, you'll find thousands of how-to books, dozens of intensive training programs, multiple lists of the "must have" qualities, and any number of dueling multistep programs to *becoming* leaders. Yet you'll be hard put to find any mention of the importance of exploring your past in the process of "becoming" a genuine leader.

Bill George, in his book *True North: Discover Your Authentic Leadership*,[4] interviewed 125 leaders from ages twenty-three to ninety-three (50 percent of them CEOs and 50 percent of them early- or mid-career leaders from for-profit and nonprofit groups). He found one common denominator: "Leadership emerged from their life stories." In short, being authentic made them more effective leaders. I smiled at that, knowing that the work my consulting group had been doing in the corporate arena had gained ground—we have found that it is *essential* to explore and evaluate one's past to succeed with integrity in the future!

It's Not Just from the Top Down!

I had been gathering material for this book with a focus on senior management, working from the premise that organizational cultures are usually shaped from the top down. Thus, my writing originally focused on stories of CEOs and other highly recognized leaders within companies that had sought consultation.

Then I asked Alan Webber, the founder of *Fast Company* magazine, to have coffee with me so I could hear his thoughts on my proposed book idea. After I expounded on the leadership analogy that "fish grow rotten from the head down," Alan interrupted me. He described how many sectors within large organizations are highly functioning and well led—despite the fact that leadership at the top level might be highly dysfunctional. These companies often "show well" because of the thriving leadership that is much farther down the organizational chart.

I had not considered this, since most of my work had been with senior-management teams on their highly troubled leadership. So I expanded from focusing only on the top-level leadership in companies and organizations to examining leadership *throughout* the organizations. From the boardroom to the stockroom, we can find both effective and dysfunctional leadership at all levels. The amount of emotional baggage brought to the workplace is not determined by a person's title, education, or salary. We often see it played out when management teams create a dysfunctional culture, because they have not faced their own unhealed emotional scars from childhood. Author Ernest Becker wrote, "If everybody lives roughly the same lies about the same things there is no one to call them liars: they jointly establish their own sanity and call themselves 'normal.'"[5] This has surely been the standard business practice in many organizations.

What I did learn, and relearned, was that when we examine our past and explore our unexamined issues, we can bring our best selves, our genuine selves, to work, and we can truly advance our career paths. We can acknowledge our strengths, our weaknesses, and our challenges that grew out of our past. This process advances not only our growth at work but also our personal growth in *all* our relationships.

When our negative behaviors remain unexplored, we can sabotage productivity and progress at significant cost to the organization. In addition, this can permanently damage the potential and success of individual employees. There is often a cancerous effect, which spreads throughout the entire organization and also affects the lives and well-being of employees' spouses, family members, and communities. The blind loyalties of the leaders within a company and their inherent values are often responsible for impeding the development of a healthy and productive workplace, because they have not faced their bondage to the past. When psychological damage or emotional wounds remain buried, psychologist Stephanie Brown has said, "The adult responds to the archaic memory of those early feelings even though they're a far way from consciousness."[6]

This bondage to the past often eclipses the organization's benefits and resilient strengths. Through the years, I have discovered that most people are quite unaware of the strengths and gifts they brought from their first families.

Little wonder then that we see some of the high costs of this lack of self-awareness—financial, family, personal relationships, community, and the organization's reputation as well! The costs of ignoring negative behaviors are high and are far beyond financial:

- A 2002 Gallup study shows that the lost productivity of disengaged employees costs the U.S. economy $370 billion *annually.*[7]

- A study by psychologist Michelle McQuaid showed that 31 percent of employees polled felt uninspired and unappreciated by their bosses; close to 15 percent felt downright miserable, bored, and lonely.[8]

- A study in the *American Journal of Preventive Medicine* estimated that the total economic cost of excessive alcohol consumption in the United States was $223.5 billion in 2006.[9]

- According to a Gallup study, 54 percent of "actively disengaged" employees believe their jobs negatively affect their physical health.[10] This is documented by an increase in absenteeism and rise in workers' compensation claims.[11]

- Studies show that the number one reason people give for leaving a job is communication issues. In other words, 64 percent of people leave because they don't feel appreciated.[12] It costs between 25 and 200 percent of an employee's salary to find and train a replacement.

- A Leadership IQ study found that 46 percent of newly hired CEOs will fail within eighteen months.[13] A 1998 study by the Center for Creative Leadership found that 40 percent of new external hires failed in eighteen months; an internal study by Heidrick & Struggles also showed that "40 percent of executives hired at the senior level are pushed out, fail or quit within 18 months."[14]

- A failed executive can cost the company as much as $1 million in direct hiring costs and in lost productivity of others in the organization, as well as decreased productivity of the next hire who assumes the role.[15]

Recently, a colleague who works for a leading international search firm that hires top-level executives for major corporations and non-profits said that his business is quite good despite the difficult economy. Surprised, I asked how this could possibly be. He replied that it was because of all the "new hires" replacing all the failed hires at the top management level. All these findings suggest the need for changes in leadership qualities.

A New Approach: Becoming a Genuine Leader

Surely replacing people is not the answer. The answer is in hiring "genuine" leaders—that is, leaders who can balance their IQ with their EQ (their emotional intelligence). This means a leader who can lead himself or herself, who is open to new ways, who is critically reflective, and who can inspire others—a person who is willing to be vulnerable when appropriate.

A person who is a genuine leader must start with self-awareness.

Self-Awareness

No matter which studies you review, you will find the words "self-awareness" at the top of the list as the most important characteristic of a genuine leader. Self-awareness requires humbly looking at yourself and your relationships with others—no matter where you are in an organization's hierarchy.

"He's been living rent-free too long in my head." A woman stood up in a seminar I was leading and stated her dilemma that simply. What a fine example of emotional baggage at work! Have you ever found yourself awake at night, obsessing about a coworker? Here are some trigger questions you can answer honestly:

- Do you have a colleague who seems to intimidate you?
- Do you find yourself using intimidating tactics in your leadership style?
- Have you ever had a boss whom you could not impress, no matter how hard you worked?
- Is there someone in your workplace to whom you took an instant dislike—for no apparent reason?
- Do you find yourself silent when witnessing unethical behaviors?
- Do you hold your staff to standards that are next to impossible?
- Do you find yourself highly reactive to others' comments before they have a chance to speak fully?
- Do you find it difficult to empathize with peers and subordinates?
- Do you find yourself silent in key decision making, then walk away angry with yourself?
- Do you find yourself questioning the ethics of a decision?
- Do you find it difficult to say with sincerity, "I'm wrong" or "I'm sorry; I made a mistake"?
- Do you find yourself silently judgmental, quietly practicing one-upsmanship as you listen to others' ideas?

A positive response to many of these questions may indicate that you are experiencing the symptoms of unnamed and/or denied emotional baggage from your own past. From wherever we lead in our organizations, we must be willing to evaluate our past to see what has shaped our leadership beliefs and attitudes, our strengths and weaknesses.

The thesis of this book is simple: the first organization we joined was our first family, our family of origin. It is in our first family that we learned how to be in a system, for good and for ill. We learned our roles there. The dynamics became natural to us as we absorbed the unspoken "rules" of the system. Some "rules" related to how we learned to show care and consideration; others related to domination and control. Yet these rules are not always arrived at logically, or even consciously.

Our first family is often the powerful, unexamined context of what shapes us—the foundation from which we are likely to view our adult relationships—in love, family, friendships, and work. Through impaired perceptions, causing unnecessary struggles, we often contribute to dysfunctional, maladaptive organizations, marriages, and family systems. Living in the shadows of our first family, we often remain hidden to ourselves, carefully disguised in well-honed false selves.

But becoming a genuine leader is very possible! Proven personal development tools are available, and learning to use them is simple, but not easy. "Becoming genuine" means entering into a vast wilderness, facing uncertainties, buried influences, and repressed feelings. It does not, however, necessarily require that you enter into long-term psychotherapy. You can start by learning from the stories of other leaders throughout this book and gaining insights into how your past affects your current communication and leadership style by using the exercises I call "Pathways for Change" at the end of each chapter. By entering into that wilderness, with other genuine leaders as role models and with some tools for building self-awareness, you hold the promise of becoming your true, genuine self.

In her book *Daring Greatly,* Brené Brown focused on the importance of being courageous enough to be vulnerable.[16] Within a short time, her book reached number one on the *New York Times* bestseller list. More and more companies today are introducing strategies that focus on the inner traits of leadership. These strategies require breaking through the denial adopted in childhood, owning our family stories, and learning to use our strengths and coping skills to become more fully human. When we can *be* genuine, we can then focus on becoming genuine leaders. We cannot express our genuine selves as a mask; we either are our real selves or we aren't.

One day while consulting with my mentor, Carl Whitaker, founder of psychodynamic family therapy, I told him about a "failed client" and expressed shame in my sense of failure. Placing his hands on my shoulders, he said, "Your problem is the same as mine—you will never become all of who you can be!" His reassuring comment went inside me and stuck like oatmeal. I felt the relief of being accepted and understood at a time when I felt most vulnerable. By becoming genuine, we become more real and, thus, we can be appreciated and, yes, loved, for who we truly are.

1

You Can and Should Go Home Again

[FINDING YOU]

*"If you cannot get rid of the family skeleton,
you may as well make it dance."*

— GEORGE BERNARD SHAW, PLAYWRIGHT WHO WON THE NOBEL PRIZE
FOR LITERATURE (1925), COFOUNDER OF THE LONDON SCHOOL
OF ECONOMICS AND POLITICAL SCIENCE (1895)

A part-time university faculty member and full-time psychologist in private practice, I sat behind the wheel to drive home after my final oral exam to defend my doctoral thesis, and suddenly said aloud, "I'm done, Dad!" My words shocked me. I was alone. My father had been dead for many years. What did this mean—"I'm done"? Where was this coming from? At the time, I was teaching a family theory course to the doctoral students at the university, so I immediately focused on my father's unspoken messages. I recalled when I was seventeen and my father presented me with my grandmother's valedictorian address. The last lines clearly emerged: "Still let me be thy child." I also remembered receiving grandmother's formal portrait, another aspect of my father's injunction to me to achieve. "You look so much like your grandmother," my dad had said. Sitting in the car that day, I smiled as I realized that a vital aspect of my academic achievement came from my father's implicit injunction. I was fascinated to recognize how this statement surfaced so clearly upon the completion of my final degree. Until then I had had no idea that I had been moving forward in the unspoken desires of my father.

Of course, I also realized that not all awareness reveals itself in such clear and pain-free ways.

Since our first family is often the unexamined context of what shapes us—the foundation from which we are likely to view our adult relationships—it is important to understand our past. A major catalyst for finding our autobiographical narrative is "going home," returning to our childhood family stories to find the vivid memories and experiences that shaped our beliefs and behaviors—both positive and negative. In psychology, we have learned that, to the extent we were reliably cared for during our early vulnerable years, we developed a bond of loyalty that connected us for the rest of our lives. In short, we grow up in our caregivers' debt, a debt repaid through enduring loyalty. Our adult behavior is often formed from allegiances to the dynamics in the family and to the unspoken commands. This loyalty is not chosen; it is not always conscious. Rather, it is a primitive response to our early-life caregivers that plays out in both positive and negative ways. These blind loyalties can take hold for many years or even a full lifetime. I often saw how these invisible or blind loyalties could not only bind someone but also hold a person hostage in some parent's or caregiver's story.

As long as we are content to stay within the confines of the memories, recollections, and conclusions about our family formed out of our childhood experiences, we are destined to continue to enact our childhood position of helpless, "no-choice reactor" to the family forces, conscious and unconscious, in all our adult relationships.

The key people in our first families often cast dominating shadows on our adult behaviors. This shadow side is hidden to us, carefully disguised in a well-honed false self. We often hear the emotional residue of our past referred to as "baggage" or "unfinished business." When it is brought into the workplace, especially at the top of an organization, we witness extremely dysfunctional, often headline-making, organizational cultures.

We all recognize that changing a work system is as difficult as changing our family systems. Anyone who has ever tried knows how challenging that can be. Yet I've learned, along with my clients, that as *we* change, so do the systems around us. My organizational work galvanized this belief: strongly motivated organizational change can only come about through personal change by the leadership within the organization.

Michael's Story

Michael, a middle-aged executive vice president in a large manufacturing company, was shocked when he appeared in his office on Monday morning only to find it was empty, except for a note on the door that his new office could be found on the third floor (no longer in the executive suite). When he got to the third floor, he immediately saw on his desk a document spelling out a six-month temporary appointment for him. Obviously Michael was still stunned when he called me (which the CEO suggested in the temporary appointment document). He was anxious to understand the recent and dramatic changes in his career, yet he was unable to reach the CEO to learn more.

In our initial interview, Michael nearly whispered, "Suddenly I'm off the senior-management team, my office moved to a lower floor, far down from my place in the executive suite!" And then he added emphatically, "And *this* is my new job description!" as he thrust toward me a few sheets of paper about a six-month, work-family planning strategy. "One of those short, time-limited initiatives," he continued. "I have six months to wrap this up and then I'll get a good benefits package." Anxiously, he continued, "All this, after almost thirty years working my way up in the company and I can't even find out why."

As I listened to a stunned Michael, I knew that something did not make sense. It was easy to empathize with him as he revealed his shocking experience, but I knew there must be much more story beyond what he was telling me. I was initially grateful and later surprised that the CEO had given me permission to talk with others on the executive team when he referred Michael to me. Michael welcomed their involvement.

I interviewed Michael's peers, subordinates, and superiors for feedback about his performance and for insight about the CEO, and I discovered people were eager to be heard. They spoke with me openly about the CEO's overuse of alcohol, his womanizing, and his crude sexist language. Knowing all would be held in confidence, most said they felt relieved that they could finally reveal this information to someone.

As far as executive committee members knew, no one had ever confronted the CEO about his inappropriate behavior. Soon I was no longer surprised at the confidence of the CEO in suggesting I speak with his executive committee members. The senior management in the firm were paid some of the top salaries in town; the senior team had golden handcuffs and were reluctant to take risks. As is often the case, the CEO had hired in his own shadow. He could trust they would not betray him by revealing his inappropriate behaviors.

I listened to accounts of senior management's drunken escapades at corporate functions, jokes that pushed the boundaries of appropriateness, and in general, a highly disrespectful work culture. I was not surprised that the people I interviewed had the same response to my questions about the unspoken rules that governed the workplace— the rules everyone followed. There seemed to be consensus about the firm's primary implicit rules:

- Check your feelings at the door.
- Never speak your truth about management's inappropriate behavior.
- Remember that the company comes first; your personal life comes second.

As Michael continued his story, he revealed that he had refused to join the other executives in their after-hours "meetings" and deal closings. He reported that he also knew several executive-level women had had affairs with senior-management team members. Recently three top-level women had approached Michael, furious about the CEO's attempted fondling and slobbery drunken kissing during a senior-management party after a deal closing. The women trusted that Michael would be a high-level executive who would be willing to take action about this. Michael admitted that they all had become accustomed to the CEO's womanizing and pornographic jokes; employees accepted his behavior as normal. Michael sadly reflected, "What really bothers me is that I witnessed his womanizing and said nothing—and I am the father of three daughters!"

He explained that he had gone immediately to the corporate legal counsel with the women's concerns. Michael took seriously his responsibility to report to the counsel what the women had told him. He was familiar with the counsel's famed reputation as a national spokesperson on corporate ethics. In their meeting, the lawyer told Michael he would "most certainly" investigate this report, but since then he had made no attempt to contact Michael or the women. I asked Michael what he knew about the lawyer's relationship to the CEO. Michael mentioned that not only was the corporate counsel the CEO's golf partner but also their families shared vacations and holidays together.

I stared into Michael's tense face and quietly asked, "And you wonder why you are on the way out?" Michael looked puzzled as he drew back in his chair. "You broke the no-talk rule," I explained. "What rule?" asked Michael. "You named the abuse," I replied. "And the one who breaks the unspoken rules is going to be punished; the system will fight to stay the same," I added. "And furthermore, you reported it to the CEO's best friend!"

I went on to explain what I meant by "rules," the *implicit, unspoken* norms that are established in all systems—family and work— reflecting who can say what to whom, who can "talk back," or who has the ear of the parent or the CEO.

We discussed the unspoken rule he broke, the implicit rule that all followed: "Don't comment on inappropriate or abusive behavior." Michael leaned forward, eyes narrowing, closely concentrating on my words. He realized that when he had done the right thing, the healthy act of integrity, he broke the no-talk rule, and quite naturally, the shame-bound system was punishing him. Although he had known about the loyal friendship of the CEO and corporate counsel, he had not seen the perils in the dual relationships—until he broke the no-talk rule. Previously, he had played it safe by keeping silent about corporate misbehaviors he himself had witnessed.

I asked Michael, "Where did you learn not to comment on your reality?" We then explored how Michael had learned to silence his reality, his perceptions. His story ran deeper than the women's sexual harassment incident at work. Michael reported that he learned early in life to cope in his emotionally abusive family by being silent in order to survive abuse. He had also internalized his alcoholic father's strong words that guided his childhood behavior: "If you talk back, you'll get it too." By age seven, he had become emotionally frozen. Now he explored highly revealing family photos and paused when he saw the face of a boy with a frightened, worried expression. He had survived, as many children of emotional or physical abuse do, by using denial ("I don't see what I see") and by telling himself that if he just kept silent in tense situations, he would not be hit or hurt.

Michael began to see clearly that he was still unconsciously loyal to the survival skills he formed so long ago—by denying his family shadow, he had corrupted his adult life, professionally and personally. I reminded him of the quotation from the Russian poet Yevgeny Yevtushenko: "Shame is the most powerful motivator of human progress."

Michael had painfully found his bedrock, his true story. He could no longer lie to himself. The learned behaviors from Michael's childhood family—bound in the shame of the unspoken rules; the addictive, compulsive behaviors; and denial—were all present in his company. Michael knew well how to endure such a system; he had found his family hiding in the shadows at work. There he had continued to play out his unconsciously enacted loyalty to his first family and its implicit rules by observing in silence.

Through his crisis, Michael began to see how the impaired, dysfunctional behaviors at work had been normalized and to learn the difference between appropriate and normalized inappropriate behaviors. At my suggestion, he began attending Adult Children of Alcoholics

(ACA) meetings at a local church. He found a sponsor in his ACA group and consulted with him. He then decided not to fight the CEO and executive committee, because his benefits package and stock options meant too much to him and his family at his age. Surely in this metropolitan city, challenging his dismissal would make big headlines, but would only sustain his pain at very high costs—both financially and emotionally. He felt handcuffed. I reminded him he could leave with dignity as we progressed toward his goal.

First, Michael spoke with the three women about the harassment; they, in turn, sought outside counsel. Michael felt guilty as he left without challenging the CEO and his board, yet this type of self-protective exit is very common. The high financial cost of legal help, along with ongoing personal pain and perhaps even media exposure, led Michael toward his chosen exit. With his wife's support, Michael proceeded carefully with an exit plan. Six months later, he announced his resignation (his "early retirement") and was able to leave with his self-esteem intact, along with a good severance package. Michael went on to establish a consulting business and recently told me that now, for the first time, he felt "real" in his work life. He had taken the steps necessary in becoming a genuine leader, one who could be authentic, confident, and approachable. With his increased self-awareness and reflection, Michael said that for the first time in his life he knew what the true meaning of integrity was.

Some may say this is not a success story. But Michael entered into the shadows of his past and faced his family shame, which had opened the door to a spiritual recovery. Michael had to "go home" to make changes in himself. It took some time for Michael to realize that, although he had never been a heavy drinker because of what he had witnessed in his early life, the effects of growing up with a "family disease" (alcoholism) were very alive in his life. Eventually, through his recovery, Michael was able to live the life of a genuine leader as a successful man, husband, father, and community contributor.

Michael's story is illustrative of many corporations achieving high financial success while simultaneously experiencing high levels of dysfunctional behaviors. From the outside, these companies look good. They "show well," with strong bottom-line performance and high-status national leaders serving on boards of directors. As long as a company is financially successful, board members seldom question the work culture.

Going Home through Guided Imagery

In my years as a corporate psychologist for a corporate consulting firm, I worked closely with executive teams to enhance their leadership. In one segment of a training seminar, I told stories of our family shadows and the importance of stepping into them. Then in a semi-darkened room, I led the typically all-male group seated in a circle through a guided imagery exercise called "Going Home," in which participants visualized themselves returning home to their early lives as a child between the age of six and ten accompanied by their adult self. The goal was to go back in time to experience the feeling world in which they grew up. As they focused on the details of their past histories, I asked them to observe who they were as children; what feelings were present as they walked through their homes; what people, pets, and childhood artifacts and collections were present. I asked them to observe and to note what feelings surfaced. They explored the homes of their childhood and the people who mattered to them. I asked them to identify the strengths they knew to be true about them at that early age. I went on to ask how they protected themselves, what "fences" they developed. Finally, I asked them to picture themselves standing in their own bedroom (or in a personal space that held their childhood artifacts). Because attendees were mostly male, I asked them to visualize their father or parent authority figure standing with hands placed on the shoulders of their young self. I then asked them to hear from their fathers or primary adult male caregiver the words they most longed to hear back at that early age.

Immediately the energy in the room shifted. I heard sniffling and saw the men attempting to brush away tears with their suit sleeves. Several wept openly. I immediately turned the lights down further, so they had time to refocus as I walked around the circle, offering Kleenex tissues. Then I slowly turned up the lights and asked them to write in their journals about the experience. Most had never experienced guided imagery before and had little awareness that these stories and images they recalled from their history might be influencing their present behavior. A few thought I had hypnotized them. In their journals, they described their reactions to the imagery, as well as reflected on how their childhood self-protection played out in their present-day leadership life. Some chose to share their discoveries with others. Most were intrigued by the experience and struck by the commonality in the messages that so many of them had longed to hear. The two most prevalent messages they had longed for as children were some form of reassurance that "Everything is going to be all right!" and "You are lovable just the way you are." They were deeply surprised to find how defenseless they felt. Eventually they were able to speak about the self-empathy they experienced as a result of "going home." Most of the men requested a tape of the guided imagery to take home to their families. Several participants called home and later reported how differently they had spoken to their children and spouses. Thawing the frozen parts of themselves had opened the door to vulnerability. The awareness from this experience led to my creating a model that could develop their emotional intelligence, that is, their feeling selves.

I followed up the imagery with individual hour-and-a-half private consultations in which each person could discuss the personal "going home" experience as it related to his or her leadership. The message was very clear: most of these executives were totally disconnected from their pasts, their own stories, and they did not realize how their present behaviors were linked to their responses from an earlier time in life. By identifying incidents from their life stories, they were able to connect their workplace behaviors with their own personal narrative. It was amazing how the stories they chose from childhood so closely paralleled what was happening in their work world.

I have found through the years that more than 85 percent of my clients have been willing to engage in this guided imagery. Through such experiences, many participants continued to take further risks in self-awareness and discovered that they could eventually take their whole selves to work, taking interpersonal risks they never would have considered earlier. They were able to take responsibility for the effect the emotional barriers they had erected had on their own lives and those of their families, their employees, and their communities. When leaders can honestly view their family culture and make the connection with how dysfunctional thinking and behaviors learned in that culture have carried over to the present, changes in their behavior at work often become immediately apparent. As they alter their communication patterns based on these insights, and as new behaviors start to take hold, work environments visibly begin to come alive with the promise of genuine leadership bringing about transformational change within the organization.

When Implicit (Unspoken) "Family Rules" Meet "Corporate Rules"

My insight into how troubled work cultures develop began with recognizing that companies and other organizations have implicit (unspoken) rules, just as our families do, regarding who can comment on what, who is the favorite, who is the scapegoat, who can speak out, who can't. When interviewing leadership teams, I typically ask, "What are the implicit, unspoken rules here that everyone has to follow?" Quite often, I hear one prevailing no-talk rule: "There's nothing going on here; don't tell anybody." This systemic rule has prevailed in many organizations for years, just as it has in families. If someone grew up in a family in which "women don't count" or "Dad must never be challenged," that person will most likely struggle with the tenacious hold these internalized messages have on adult relationships.

"On a Clear Day You Can See Your Mother!"

Once in the late 1970s, I saw this title on the marquee of an improvisational theater in Minneapolis and I smiled. What a descriptor for our unconscious loyalties to our families, for how our first family is often the powerful, unexamined context of what shapes us and our perceptions. Lurking in the shadows of our work cultures where the no-talk rule is built into the system, these loyalties can contribute to compulsive work patterns of perfectionism and of abusive, disrespectful behaviors. We see these patterns in offices and boardrooms in many forms—poor boundaries, secrets, sarcasm, cynicism, dishonesty, gossip, greed, silence, reactivity, resentments, jealousy, and deference to authority. The list is long. These behaviors are of course often unwittingly and unknowingly performed—and with the rule established for not calling them out, they will continue until a crisis intervenes.

Obviously we bring our family's strengths to work as well. Although these assets can serve to sustain an outwardly successful organization, they are typically eclipsed by the shame-bound dysfunctional behaviors, especially at the executive level, where leaders are more insulated from criticism.

Alcoholism and Drug Abuse Take a Toll

Probably no other secrets are less talked about among leaders than alcoholism and drug abuse—both as a legacy from first families and in their own lives. One in twelve adults abuses alcohol or is alcohol-dependent.[1] Among those affected are executives, surgeons, pilots, and other successful professionals. Alcoholism has played an important role in the lives of many of our leaders. Some studies have shown that 19.5 percent of U.S. alcoholics are middle-aged, well-educated, with stable jobs and families. More than one-third of these people have a multigenerational history of alcoholism. According to the Substance Abuse and Mental Health Services Administration, substance abuse and other addictions cost $81 billion in lost productivity a year. It is easy to understand how much more motivated executives are to hide their abuse, and unfortunately, how they usually are able to hide such behavior much more easily than their hourly employees can.

This isn't a problem only in the executive suite. In the late 1980s and early 1990s, we saw a high number of pilots fired or imprisoned for abuse of alcohol while flying. The requirement for pilots is to be alcohol-free for twenty-four hours before they fly. I recall a coaching client, Tom, who came in one day in a highly agitated state. When I asked him what was bothering him, he said he had to confess that he had problems with drinking and with women. He had been flying intoxicated three times in the last month and was frightened that he might cause a crash. "The problem, you see, is that my airline does not have any way to get help," he explained. "If you are found drinking, you are permanently grounded. Period. It's over. I cannot afford to give up my job. I am afraid to go to AA for fear that some of our airline customers might see me in the group." Tom was living in daily, chilling fear. He agreed to go across town to a Twelve Step meeting once a day for thirty days (except when flying), and he made great progress. At the same time, his airline finally announced it was offering help to its addicted pilots after three of its pilots went to prison for flying drunk. A leading treatment facility provided help for the airline's employees and, within a few years, the airline received awards for its progressive attitude toward the disease of alcoholism.

Although a corporate middle manager or executive probably isn't putting people's lives at risk with his or her substance abuse, *BtoB* studies have shown that the person is contributing to millions of dollars in lost productivity.[2] Like the pilots, many people in positions of power—or in positions on the ladder to power—fear the stigma of addiction and, even if they are aware that their drinking or drug use is getting out of control, they won't seek help. It's been well established that addiction is a biological disorder that can be treated, but still, the shame and secrecy that is associated with addiction can prevail in many corporate work environments, especially when the people involved have alcohol and drug abuse in their family histories. Often fellow employees and even supervisors of people with an alcohol or drug problem won't encourage them to get help because of the no-talk rule and ignorance of addiction as a treatable disease. Supervisors and employees may even cover for them, further contributing to the problem and putting their company, and even the person whom they're covering for, at risk. The decision to resist change and, therefore, to prevent growth has dramatic consequences. Often we discover we have maintained our role as no-choice reactor to the forces, conscious and unconscious, in our workplace. We do this through remaining in the shadows of our first families, shutting down our emotions, and conforming to rules, including remaining silent when workplace dysfunctional behaviors, such as sexual harassment or addiction, run rampant. As I've learned using the "Going Home" guided imagery exercise described earlier, when we have the courage to make the passage back in time as an adult and we uncover our shadows, we can leave behind misplaced childhood loyalty to people in our families who cast those shadows, and we can create a new adult identity. This then allows us to look at the familiar scenes of workplace life through a different lens, an adult lens. Focusing through an adult lens, we can identify ways to break through the limits and emotional shackles imposed by the past.

Pathways for Change

This section includes a family genogram, family history, and the "Going Home" guided imagery. These exercises provide useful tools for you to continue to explore the ideas from this chapter.

Family Genogram

Family genograms are often a first step for leaders to identify their family history. A family genogram is more than a family tree; it provides a pictorial representation of your relationships to family members. This representation of relationships allows you to visualize the psychological patterns and tendencies that inform your current relationships. When leaders can explore their own life crucibles by studying their genograms, they make remarkable progress in self-awareness.

The genogram, along with a series of questions, can awaken dormant feelings and observations. Also, this process can be the source for identifying where the pruning of that family tree needs to happen.

Use the symbols in the key below to create your own genogram. Also provided is an example of a genogram on page 15.

Genogram Symbols

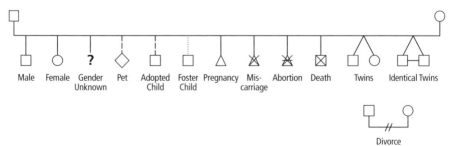

Genogram Example

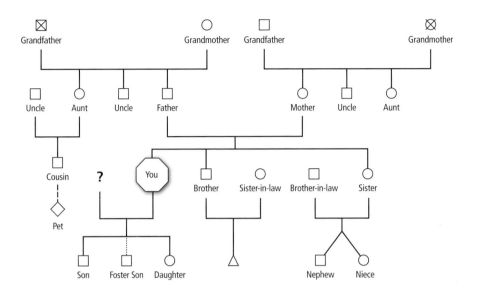

If you'd like to learn more about genograms, you can read the following book: McGoldrick, Monica, Randy Gerson, and Sueli Petry, *Genograms: Assessment and Intervention,* 3rd ed., New York: W.W. Norton, 2008.

Instead of the genogram, or in addition to it, the enneagram model of nine interconnected personality types may be a helpful concept to you. A number of books and online resources on enneagrams are available. Another helpful tool is the Myers Briggs Type Indicator, which should be done with a professional.

Family History

Review your family history by answering the following questions.

1. When and where were you born? How did your family come to live there? What is your earliest childhood memory?

2. Describe the personalities of your family members—parents, siblings, grandparents.

3. What is your full name? Why did your parents select this name for you? Did you have a nickname?

4. Describe your parents' relationship. Describe your relationship with your siblings.

5. Were there any divorces or adoptions in your family?

6. What family issues were known and spoken of (suicides, health issues, abuse, alcoholism, mental illness, etc.)? How did your family talk about these issues?

7. How did your family members manage their emotions?

8. What were the family rules that everyone had to follow?

9. What income strata were you raised in: an upper-, middle-, or low-income family?

10. What was your family's professed religion? Were family members actively involved? Did they encourage you to be involved?

11. Name three words that describe your family's strengths. (These are your inherited gifts.)

12. How did your family discipline children? Was it fair?

13. What were the family secrets (for example, Uncle Joe was indicted for fraud and put in prison)?

14. What were the family taboos (for example, no discussion of sexuality)?

15. What cut-offs (physical or emotional withdrawal) or fusions (emotional "oneness" or too much togetherness) did you see in your family?

16. What were some of your inherited myths about your family?

17. How did your family recognize, praise, and/or acknowledge your achievements?

"Going Home" Guided Imagery

Many people who have experienced this guided imagery have asked to have a recorded copy. I include the text here so you can record it in your own voice if you wish:

> Seated comfortably and with your eyes closed, breathe deeply and let all tension fall from your shoulders. Be aware of all that your senses bring to you. Pay attention to what you see, what you hear, what you taste, what you smell, what you are touching. Now, paying careful attention to your breathing, also pay careful attention to your feelings as you continue to let go. Pay attention to all the details of your breathing. You see yourself standing at the top of a winding staircase, but you are not alone. You are a child between six and ten years old; you are not going home alone. Your adult self is accompanying you. Slowly, slowly, breathe in . . . breathe out. . . . See yourself walking down into your past, accompanied by your adult you.
>
> Now you are at the bottom of the stairwell, and there before you stands the home or dwelling in which you lived at this particular age. Be aware of how you feel as you face this part of your past. Slowly, you see yourself, holding the hand of your adult self, walking toward the entrance you most likely would have used at this time in your life. You open the door and enter. You are not here to work anything through, just to observe. Who might be home? Is there a pet in the family? You walk through the various rooms and take note of any feelings that arise in you. Take note and continue to the kitchen. Have a seat at the table. Who else might be with you?

Pay attention to your feelings. Are you aware of any memorable scenes here?

Now leave this space and go to your room, or your part of the room that held your memorabilia, your things, the artifacts of your childhood. This may include puzzles, games, books, athletic equipment, hobby materials, and such. Just observe your childhood past and any feelings that come.

As you take all this in, see yourself sitting on your bed or your sleeping area. You see your adult parent or caretaker enter the room. This parent or caretaker puts his or her hands on your shoulders and tells you what you always longed to hear. You are filled with the feelings that come with the messages longed for so many years ago. Feeling the protection of your adult self at your side, you can acknowledge (or not) anything you might want to say in return.

Again, paying attention to your feelings, you make your way through your home or dwelling and exit through the same door. You will leave the door ajar, knowing you might want to return there in the future. Feeling the loving companion at your side, you slowly make your way away from your home, move toward the stairwell, and begin the climb up from the past to the present, to this room. Now, focusing on your breathing and your feelings as you reach the top of the stairs, gently open your eyes and be aware of all that surrounds you. And now take a notebook and a pen or pencil and write what message you heard from your parent or guardian at this early age.

A book for women—and men—in handling stress when "going home" is *The Dance of Anger: A Woman's Guide to Changing the Patterns of Intimate Relationships* by Harriet Lerner (New York: HarperCollins, 1985).

2

Facing Shame and Denial about the Past
[SETTING BOUNDARIES IN THE PRESENT]

"In the middle of the road of my life I awoke in a dark wood where the way was wholly lost."

— DANTE, ITALIAN POET OF THE MIDDLE AGES, AUTHOR OF *DIVINE COMEDY*

When I was a young girl listening to evening radio shows, one of our family favorites was *The Shadow*. The show opened with an eerie voice asking, "Who knows what evil lurks in the hearts of men? The Shadow knows." What stayed with me through the years was the "knowing" of The Shadow.

Dictionaries offer several definitions of *shadow*. Here are some of the most relevant definitions for our purposes:

- the rough image cast by an object blocking rays of illumination

- a phantom, a ghost

- either a dark part of something or an area of complete darkness

If we're lucky, our legacy from our families for how we live and work with people includes lessons about looking for the good in others, praising them for their actions, and participating fully with them in projects in a cooperative manner. It is in our family's shadow side, however, where the dysfunctional beliefs and behaviors lurk, which are often hidden, locked in the family's denial. Lying at the core of the shadow side is shame. In our book, *Facing Shame: Families in Recovery,* coauthor Merle Fossum and I defined *shame* this way:

Shame is more than loss of face or embarrassment. Shame is an inner sense of being completely diminished or insufficient as a person. It is the self judging the self. A moment of shame may be humiliation so painful or an indignity so profound that one feels one has been robbed of her or his dignity or exposed as basically inadequate, bad, or worthy of rejection. A pervasive sense of shame is the ongoing premise that one is fundamentally bad, inadequate, defective, unworthy, or not fully valid as a human being.[1]

Shame lies at the core of the self. French philosopher Jean Paul Sartre described shame as "an immediate shudder which runs through me from head to foot without any discursive preparation."[2] As they begin to enter their shadows, many people discover that shame indeed provokes a bodily response. Some people feel a tightening in their stomach, others experience high anxiety, and most freeze. Words fall away. Sheldon experienced much the same.

Sheldon's Leadership Change

Sheldon had been the head of his division in a midsize manufacturing firm for fifteen years. When we came into the firm to do leadership training, he learned about his shadow side—his misguided loyalties—from his peers and from direct-report feedback (i.e., feedback from those who worked under him). He was stunned to hear highly critical feedback from his senior-management team. Initially, he felt he couldn't move, not even to reply. When he recovered himself and was offered the opportunity to explore his past to reflect on what had shaped his leadership, he was eager for the opportunity. Now in his late forties, he realized that he was at a crux in his career regarding promotions.

As a young boy, Sheldon had learned to be loyal to his father's intimidation, impatience, and anger. His father's injunction to the eldest of his three sons was to be a leader, for Sheldon to fulfill his father's *own* dreams. Consequently, Sheldon always felt like a failure; he was never good enough. His direct reports' feedback revealed they did not trust him and found him unreliable. It took little encouragement for a fearful but curious Sheldon to be willing to step into the shadows of his past.

As Sheldon walked into his shadow, he found an angry, resentful boy. He realized that he had learned to manipulate others in order to survive his father's dominating personality. He was able to win his mother's sympathy; together he and his mother often talked behind his father's back. He never realized in those early years that he was the receptacle for his mother's frustrations. It had been decided: Dad was an ogre; his abusive anger was to be avoided at all costs. Sheldon had never realized that he was his mother's "intimate other." She would wait for him to come home from his activities and pour her heart out to him. He began to see that she had used him as her confidant; he began to see why his wife had resented his mother through the twelve years of their marriage.

He then began a long journey home, resigning his role as his mother's chosen child and standing up to his father and letting him know how his behavior had affected him. Sheldon had not realized how he had been held hostage in his parents' marriage dynamic. Knowing the source of his inherited shame, he was able to make behavioral changes that were sincere and trustworthy. Within only eight months, his follow-up assessments from his direct reports had changed dramatically in a positive direction. Sheldon showed his direct reports a quote from Arthur Miller's play *After the Fall*:

> I dreamed I had a child, and even in the dream I saw it was my life. And it was an idiot, and I ran away. But it always crept onto my lap again, clutched at my clothes. Until I thought, if I could kiss it, whatever in it was my own, perhaps I could sleep, and I bent to its broken face, and it was horrible . . . but I kissed it. I think one must finally take one's life in one's arms. . . .[3]

This Arthur Miller excerpt clearly expresses what Sheldon experienced as he took his life into his own arms. He said he finally was feeling free from his shame-bound past.

Tony's Leadership Came with Self-Doubt

Ethnic shame has also caused many leaders to "take one's life in one's arms." Tony Gerlicz is one of those leaders.

When I first met Tony Gerlicz, he was the Head Learner at Monte del Sol Charter School, grades seven to twelve, in Santa Fe, New Mexico. I had gone in to do some pro bono coaching, but I was immediately drawn into the sphere surrounding this remarkable leader. When Peter Senge, the director of the Society of Organizational Learning at MIT's Sloan School of Management, asked where he could find a good "learning organization" in Santa Fe, he was directed to Monte del Sol and Tony. Of course, Peter was delighted to see "Head Learner" on the sign over Tony's door. After interviewing faculty, board, and students, I learned that Tony's leadership was very highly respected; all he needed was some calendar coaching for his very full life. Tony's leadership style struck me as very positive; he was empathic, yet structured, creative, inclusive, and he had all the leadership qualities I had been emphasizing in my client work. He was able to be vulnerable with the students and the faculty, a most positive role model for the students.

When I first met Tony, his school was in a shopping center, having moved out of space in a Boys and Girls Club. To recruit a diverse population, Tony went to the trailer parks of south Santa Fe, knocking on doors, talking in Spanish with parents about the school. Soon the school had a population that was 51 percent Hispanic. And in a state where schools rank among the lowest nationally, 95 percent of the students in Monte del Sol went on to further education at trade schools, community colleges, and universities.

Tony was and is a creative leader. He instituted a mentorship program in the school, where every student was mentored in a mutual field of interest; each student was required to have two years of mentorship in any field they chose. The curriculum had arts in every area. Since this was a charter school with a lottery system, I was not surprised to learn that for sixty new places in the school, there were six hundred applicants.

The faculty were all highly committed and truly worked as a system. The school's foundation board caught the enthusiasm, and soon a new building appeared on land donated by a friendly developer.

At first glance, you might think Tony had always been a natural, genuine leader. But Tony had to work through some conflicts in his own family crucible. He was born to immigrant parents from Poland who came to the United States via Argentina when Tony was four. He and his brother had to learn English immediately; his parents, both educated (his mother at the Sorbonne and his father at Warsaw's Polytechnic University), began speaking English at home so their boys could learn the language quickly. The family was poor and lived in an enclave in Pennsylvania where the reputation of Poles was as uneducated people working in the trades and in the coal mines. He said he always felt "lesser than."

This is where Tony's immigrant self-doubt and uncertainty took hold. He said he always had a sense of humility and uncertainty even though he was a strong athlete and a good student and he had good social skills. Growing up, Tony's father could never understand the poor attitude toward Poles; at home Tony's parents taught him the glory of Poland. Yet Tony saw and felt that the movers and shakers were of "a certain type" and his family was not a part of that. He thought those leadership roles were for people much more privileged and competent than he was.

When Tony looked into his shadow, he saw how large his mother loomed; she spoke five languages and was a strong woman who dominated his father. He said it was hard for him to fathom his mother's horrific stories of Nazi-occupied Poland.

Tony also realized that his mother, underneath her confident facade, was very insecure. With her many competencies and her remarkable life experiences, Tony wondered how she could be insecure.

He said that when he looked at her, he felt that he could never be that accomplished.

I asked Tony about his first leadership experiences and learned they did not occur until he became a teacher. This surprised me because he was seen as such a revered and respected leader. Tony's success as a leader began in his first teaching position in Nido de Aguilas International School, Santiago, Chile. There he led committees, got people to work together, and soon received positive feedback for his leadership skills. His upward path continued back in the United States in both inner-city schools and elite private schools. Despite all his successes, the self-doubt, the shadow of his past, clung to him.

After serving four years at Monte del Sol, Tony went to head the American School of Warsaw in Poland. Throughout his life, his mother's stories had haunted him. The stories were so hard to believe—traveling many miles through sewers, helping prisoners over the mountains to freedom, being arrested by the Gestapo, experiencing subsequent torture, and escaping. Although these stories seemed unfathomable to Tony in the United States, he heard many similar stories while he was in Poland. As he retraced his family's history, Tony was soon able to understand at a deep personal level the impact on her, and eventually on him, of his mother's history and the burden of the stories she carried from her past. He said that knowing now how his mother's secret pain had affected him, he was released from the hidden shame he had carried and was no longer a prisoner of these family stories.

Throughout his career, Tony was always authentic. His humility had served him well. With additional insight into his family's past, he evolved naturally into what we would call a genuine leader.

Naming Shame

When I was coaching an executive team for a large company, I noted that one of the owners, Ned, an extroverted, gregarious personality, often fell silent in his partners' meetings. In a one-on-one personal coaching session, I asked him what happened to him in those meetings. "I'm not sure," he replied, "but I know there are times I just can't speak." Then I asked him to give a name to his shame, and as though he had always known it, he replied, "Choker." He explained, tears welling in his eyes, "I always feel my shame when I'm with the other guys; I don't feel I deserve to be with them." It did not take too many coaching sessions for Ned to recognize Choker when he appeared. He could then mentally say to himself, "Hello, Choker; I'm busy now." By identifying and making room for the reality of his physical experience of shame, he could dismiss it for that time and contribute to the conversations.

When he was able to explore his family history and face the reality of his early childhood story—a story of a constant feeling of inferiority in the face of brutal competition with two older, high-achieving brothers (both Harvard grads while Ned attended a state university)—Ned could release the defenses that had protected him for so long. He also developed a deep sense of empathy through insight into his need to project a false sense of confidence, as he recognized the masks or false selves of his direct reports and business partners, and as a result, he was able to work with them more compassionately and effectively. He experienced firsthand how denial and shame walk hand in hand. Ned had lived with a lifetime of denial about his legacy of shame instilled through the dynamics of his family life, and for many years it had protected him.

The Positive Function of Denial

Denial blinds people to what happens right in front of them, allowing them to create and sustain a false version of reality. Denial diminishes life by blocking from consciousness important information from our past that still has an impact on our feelings and behavior in the present. However, we must remember that denial is a major coping mechanism for young children raised in highly dysfunctional or maladaptive families with systems of perfectionism, alcoholism, drug abuse, emotional and sexual abuse, or family violence. Our workplace cultures replicate the emotional processes that those in authority, that is, the parent figures, impose on those with less power, that is, the children. Most management teams do not plan to create dynamics that operate from abusive power; they simply act out what they had inherited as "normal." The resultant damage is often smoothed over with a tacit veneer of normalcy. Keeping these unresolved conflicts in the shadows results in a culture of false selves meeting false selves, creating a leadership dynamic driven by shame and secrecy.

In the introduction, I said that the unhealthy behaviors resulting from denial can sabotage productivity, eventually affecting the bottom line, with potential damage to an organization's reputation and standing in the community. The psychological impact on employees, and even their family members, can have long-term consequences that can compromise their quality of life and motivation to contribute to the organization's ongoing success. Lost work from sick time taken for stress-related illnesses can also cost both employees and the organization.

Marianne (Molly) Kaufmann is an applied behavioral scientist with a unique role managing the training, talent, and organizational development functions of a growing government agency in a large city. She recently contacted me regarding her remarkable findings related to the impact of shame on one of her teams and how her ongoing work uncovered this dynamic throughout the agency. When she made the connection that she was working with a shame-bound organization, she actively engaged both with whole teams and individual leaders and managers on the shame patterns they had replicated from their past into their workplace. I was surprised that she could have this kind of success with an issue this complex and usually well protected, so I asked, "How did you ever get them to name their shame?" Following lots of experimentation, Molly used a combination of two major tools to find what worked in this difficult area of leadership and team development.

The first tool was the EQ in Action Profile. This tool, created by Learning in Action Technologies and based on the science of the emotional intelligence quotient (EQ), revealed a high shame profile for many of her clients, with especially high concentrations of shame on some teams.

Measuring emotional intelligence is an evolving science. The ability to not only perceive your own emotions but also to understand where they come from and, therefore, to manage them and express them in a constructive way is especially relevant in workplace settings. It's particularly valuable for leaders to develop the basic self-awareness that allows them to regulate their emotions motivated by empathy for others' feelings and a desire to be socially adept in working with people toward common goals. This can be very difficult when a shame-based system, whether in a family or in the workplace, creates restrictive rules around even acknowledging real feelings, much less encouraging their honest expression.

In using the emotional intelligence tool with her clients, Molly reported that shame "had become systemic; it was throughout the organization." Individuals throughout the agency explored what was going on in their patterns of family life and how that was showing up at work. They used a family genogram workbook, Molly's second major tool, to explore their family patterns that have been passed along generation to generation. As a result of this work, several team members are now using their genogram to explore their shame history, often along with exploring the dynamics of shame through reading and discussing what they're learning with family members and coworkers.

Molly's work included discussions on family rules and how they parallel unwritten rules at work. In addition, Molly is an advocate for educating her clients. She believes that people can self-direct their lives better if they learn theory and apply it in all systems of their lives, whether in work, family, community, or spiritual life. Therefore, she gave them many other reading assignments—including *Facing Shame: Families in Recovery* to learn about dynamics of shame, Dan Siegel's *The Developing Mind*[4] to explore attachment theory, the works of Brené Brown, and literature on Bowen family systems theory (developed by Dr. Murray Bowen to give people the knowledge and tools to differentiate themselves from their family systems)—to help her clients more fully understand how systems trigger and sustain predictable patterns of behavior. All of these resources helped Molly's clients to further develop an authentic self.

Learning in Action Technologies in Seattle, Washington, the firm that developed the EQ in Action Profile, has given this test to more than thirteen thousand individuals—many of them in top leadership roles—throughout the United States, with some participation from other countries throughout the world. Those who took the test learned about the connection between high shame scores and self-centeredness.

Through the years I almost always found that most narcissistic leaders had a high degree of shame in their stories. When they are finally able to name the rules of shame, they have been able to break those same rules through their individual and team work. Molly's experimentation has led her to develop a powerful tool in working with individuals in shame-bound organizational systems: EQ Coaching Circles. The circles were invented to give individuals in a small-group setting an opportunity to deepen their understanding of themselves and to break some of the denial, perfectionism, and other inherited dynamics from their families. Through this process of meeting monthly for six to nine months, individuals learn both to be coached and to coach authentically. Although the circles have many positive impacts for circle members, their main purposes are learning to lead from any position in an organization with intent, clear thinking, human connection, and reduced anxiety.

Molly also uses the works of Bill George, whose books have made the connection between family history and workplace behavior more palatable for members of her circles. She has incorporated *Finding Your True North: A Personal Guide* by Bill George, Andrew McLean, and Nick Craig in her private coaching with individuals and in the coaching circles, offering two exercise options:

1. Do an autobiography, going back as far as you can remember and writing about your stories with your first family, or, if you

prefer, write a blog. For example, one circle member has started a blog of her life that she shares with her family, often collecting their stories along with hers.

2. Read *Finding Your True North: A Personal Guide* (the more popular of the two options),[5] which helps to guide people, especially if they are more reluctant to take a backward look at their growing-up years to understand and use the gifts of their authentic self.

Molly's coaching circles occur mostly at a grass-roots level of experimentation with volunteer teams and organization members. Although she insists that this work can only be voluntary (for example, you can never "make" others face their shame, their past, and other things that lurk in the shadows of their life experience), it has become one of two options that individuals—such as senior managers, supervisors, auditors, and project managers—can select as a capstone course to earn a certificate in management excellence.

Molly Kaufmann developed EQ Coaching Circles as a way to cultivate emotional intelligence in organizations. The circles help each circle member meet unique goals that go beyond the normal formats, styles, and subject matters of traditional business coaching or training. Circles consist of committed peers who meet regularly to learn and grow from each other in relationships as equals within the circle. The program is designed to help individuals explore together their individual journeys into the past—to share, bear witness, and help each other with life's entrapments or "hooks" and provocations or "triggers" that show up at work. By becoming self-aware and learning strategies from each other and the facilitator for coping with life's hooks and triggers, members ideally will advance their performance in life and work.

Through Molly's creative work, her clients begin to break the rules of the shame-bound system and are able to move forward.

In *Facing Shame: Families in Recovery,* Merle Fossum and I outlined the rules of the shame-bound system:

- *Control.* Be in control of all behavior and interaction.

- *Perfection.* Always be "right": do the "right" thing. Be admired. Look good.

- *Blame.* If the unexpected occurs or you're surprised, blame yourself or someone else. Remember, you're either totally responsible or it's someone else's fault.

- *Denial.* Deny feelings, especially vulnerable feelings of anxiety, fear, loneliness, sadness, or grief.

- *Unreliability.* Expect little of people; don't count on constancy in relationships.

- *Incompleteness.* Be sure you never complete a transaction; keep the anxiety going.[6]

It's often pretty self-evident when these family rules of shame have infiltrated an organization. When I train professionals and ask them to communicate using only the rules of shame, I've found that within minutes the groups experience the shame that before had been only a concept. The exercise has been so powerful in our seminars that we do not use this approach unless we know we will be with the team for at least two to three days.

Some of these shame rules were in play among the family members of our next example.

The Family Business Story of John and Sue

When I initially met these fifth-generation family business owners on the West Coast, I thought Sue was the CEO. She was poised, confident, and in charge. I was surprised when I learned that pale, hunched-over John was the CEO. I also met with the family governing board: all five children including John and Sue, and their father, Daniel, who actually ran the company. I had asked them to conduct their meeting as usual, explaining that I would then give them feedback on what I observed. After giving my feedback, I left the room so they could decide whether they thought my observations were useful and whether they wanted to work with me. It had been a good session; we agreed we could work together. I had noted that sibling tensions were high and trusted that we would unravel the history behind that.

On my flight afterward, something troubled me as I reviewed the family history I had gathered that afternoon. When I arrived home, I realized no one had mentioned their mother—and just as important, *I had not asked!* I called back immediately to ask Sue about her. "Oh, she died," Sue said. "When was that?" I asked. "Oh, twenty-five years ago," she replied. "Of what?" I asked. "Alcoholism" was the reply.

Then, like a bolt of lightning, it hit me. I remembered that I had smelled alcohol in John's coffee cup in the boardroom at 10 a.m. I also recalled how he held on to his coffee cup throughout the meeting. I realized I had immediately bought into the family system. By not inquiring, I had by omission adhered to their no-talk rule about their mother; I had immediately dismissed the evidence I had seen of this missing dynamic. The loyalty to their family rule of "don't ever mention alcohol abuse" had created strained, emotionally dishonest conversations in their meetings.

When I returned to meet with the family again, I asked permission to get individual interviews. When I asked Daniel about his son's drinking, he said that he knew his son was an active alcoholic and that he worried about John's driving around town with his three grade-school-aged children. I asked, "Do you realize your son is killing himself?" He sheepishly replied, "Well, I thought if we kept him busy in the business that we could keep track of him and protect the family." I looked him straight in the eye and said, "But you also recall that this is how your wife died; you are all colluding in his disease." He hung his head, then looking back up, asked, "Can you help us?"

My original contract was for succession planning for the family business. Yet I knew that unless we addressed the shame-based no-talk issues, we could not do what needed to be done. They all agreed. In an unusual move, the siblings agreed to my unorthodox request that I wear another hat to accomplish their goal for their brother. In my follow-up interviews, we decided that an intervention was needed.

All were present at the intervention, including John's wife, who was simultaneously anxious and fearful that he would refuse. In the meeting, the family expressed their sincere care and concern and told stories of dangerous occurrences related to John's drinking. John heard their deep concern and pleas. He entered a treatment center for alcoholism and began a solid recovery program.

I was then able to put on my consultant hat once again, and we were able to get on with the succession work in an honest, thoughtful way. Because of the down-turned economy, major business decisions had to be made. Now, all were present at the table, making wise decisions. John, as of this writing, has been sober for more than ten years. John's siblings took time to trust again and not become fearful at company and family events where alcohol might be served. But change at work does not mean that changes will come automatically at home. It takes time for the system to adapt to the changed, respectful behaviors.

As We Change, So Does the System Around Us—with Time!

Often changes at work come relatively easily if the key people in the organizational "family" system are committed to change. Transferring that learning to the family at home can take much longer. Frank was the head of a national nonprofit organization, someone who truly "got it" and was determined to make real changes after moving through a series of training seminars and achieving high success in his organization. Having faced his past, he was excited to share his new awareness and translate his insights into a fresh outlook on parenting. But his wife, Stephanie, who had been loyal to him through his years of complaining, was skeptical. Stephanie was furious when Frank said no to her demand that he "beat these kids for their bad behavior while you were gone." Frank decided to talk with them instead; he had committed to end any family abuse. As might be expected, Stephanie was slow to trust these changes in their entrenched family system. Frank felt conflicted with his work-family differences. The family system was not yet ready to change, making it clear that he had to slowly introduce his new behaviors into the home. Frank and his wife entered a couples communication class, and they both reinforced the new patterns Frank had learned. Eventually they were able to share their life-changing patterns; however, this took several years with many speed bumps along the way. What was important was their realization that a process of change could be set in motion, that a process of reconnecting—to themselves, to family members—could be enacted.

Shadows Lurk and Return

Even when there has been a solid investment of time and energy in understanding one's past, the shadow can reappear. Such was the story of Sam.

When I met Sam two years after our original coaching work and consulting with his small family business, I learned about how persistently family ghosts can reappear. In his initial work, Sam had explored his first family and was able to identify the family ghosts that were haunting him. Now something seemed different.

Sam was sitting upright at his round office table, leaning back in what appeared to be an uncomfortable position and holding on to the chair's armrests as though to anchor himself. Sam's company president, Charlie, sat across the table from him. I had positioned myself in the middle.

They had agreed to call me to facilitate a difficult conversation after a flurry of emails had flooded the system. The emails were a response to a mandate that Sam had sent to the entire executive team. I began by asking Sam how he chose to send this "mandate" that had caused so much reaction in his senior team. Something had not seemed right. Sam typically worked hand in hand with Charlie since they had worked together on their cultural transformation. Charlie had responded strongly and negatively to Sam's edict about totally changing the course of their strategic plan, which they had all worked together to develop. The mandate caused them all to return to old behaviors of gossiping, reacting with strong emotions, and "triangling" conversations to include Charlie, who had eventually become the champion of the entire team.

Since I had history with Sam and knew how his domineering father had loomed over him, casting a giant shadow, I immediately wondered whether his father were somewhere in this picture. I knew that his father still held the controlling stock in the company and was particularly cynical about any new projects, such as the plan the team had developed.

I asked Sam where this had come from and whether he had spoken with his father. He said no but then said, "Well, I did talk with my board." It turned out that his board had questioned the strategic plan, which triggered the old messages from Sam's past—the fear that his father would influence the board to withdraw funds. So in an attempt to please his board and out of fear of his father's intrusion, Sam had sent the rigid, formal "mandate" to his senior team, telling them that they would need to create an entirely new plan. The language was crisp and clear, sounding almost militaristic. It was not the voice of the Sam that the team had grown to trust and respect.

The team members, shocked, had all gone to Charlie to ask what was going on. They were angry, confused, and uncertain about how to proceed. It was not like their CEO to suddenly pull rank after they had worked so long and so hard to build a real decision-making team. They said they felt betrayed.

My step-by-step questioning of Sam led to his confession that he had acted too quickly. He owned the fact that he was trying to please his father and his board rather than standing up for what he and his senior team had developed. By owning his awareness, and apologizing to Charlie, Sam was able to go back to the team and tell them the truth, showing his full humanness in his vulnerability and apologizing for not taking a stand in support of the "we" team they had grown. Sam had indeed grown up in a family with very blurred personal boundaries, with his father crossing the generational line and constantly forging his style onto Sam's decision making. Sam had been "hooked" one more time, but this time he was able to name it and resolve it quickly by being vulnerable and honest with his team.

Blurred Boundaries

Lucy was sent to me because of her inappropriate behaviors with many of the men in her office. She was known as a highly productive leader with a charming style. When she came for her first appointment with me, I greeted her at my office door. She said hello, strode past me across my office, and sat on top of my desk, where she picked up the phone to make a call. I knew immediately that Lucy had boundary issues and that she most likely had been personally violated.

Lucy did not have common sense about where she ended and someone else began. I took note that we would need to address her style of dress. She wore a very low-cut blouse. I learned later that many of her colleagues snickered about her behind her back. Later, I pointed out to Lucy that she had the right to dress as she chose, but that there was an expectation of "business" or "business casual" in her office. Lucy knew why she was to consult with me; she was a remarkable flirt. Several men had complained to the human resources staff about Lucy sending notes that violated their personal boundaries, standing too close in interactions, and going out drinking with new executive team members.

In my second meeting with her, we explored her family tree. Using the genogram, Lucy identified the marriages, divorces, deaths, diseases, ethnicity, and dysfunctional relationships, all with symbols showing the connections through the generations. When I asked about addiction, Lucy highlighted three generations of alcohol addiction. As Lucy began to explore the threads of addiction with its scores of boundary violations, she recalled her father's "sloppy wet" kisses when he was drunk, his lack of modesty, and his emotional and intellectual violations in discussing with her his marital sex life. It did not take long for Lucy to see that "apples grow on apple trees." Lucy had learned to sexualize her behaviors, just as her father had exhibited.

She knew there were secrets about her mother's affairs and her father's cheating, all wrapped in the secrecy often seen in a shame-bound alcoholic family. Lucy said in our next interview that she knew she too was an addict. "I just can't stay away from the guys!" she blurted. Lucy chose to enter a treatment program to focus on her sexual addiction. She needed additional support so that in time she could be seen with new eyes by her fellow employees. With the help of a therapist, she was able to make major changes in how she behaved.

Both Sam and Lucy were held hostage by family boundary invasions. All too often we hear, "He doesn't have any boundaries!" What people typically are referring to are intrusive behaviors—intellectual, emotional, or physical, or perhaps all three.

In Sam's case, his father used to interrupt all Sam's statements and shame him so that he never quite trusted his own perceptions. When Sam saw the "zipper" boundary model that follows, he could see how his father had "unzipped" him and entered into his intellectual and emotional space.

Our personal boundary is the protective screen that develops around the self to hold the growing self, our budding ego, intact. It encompasses our most inner space, our space through which we interpret what our senses bring us. As children grow, they form an identity and develop boundaries to separate the self from the rest of the world. These boundaries provide a sense of security to children and protect their innocence. Later our boundaries determine our sense of self-esteem, our self-confidence, and our sense of control over our lives. With clearly defined boundaries, we know our own thoughts and feelings.

In dysfunctional families, our boundaries become blurred because of the generational crossovers of parents through *boundary invasion* or *boundary neglect.* When a child grows up with respect for the growing self—intellectually, emotionally, and physically—he or she grows up with the "zipper" (locus of control) on the inside and can self-regulate behaviors, thoughts, and feelings. When a child has had boundary invasions or neglect through intellectual abuse, emotional abuse, or physical abuse, the child grows up with the zipper on the outside—allowing others to "unzip" their boundaries and enter their personal space intellectually, emotionally, or physically. Sam's story reveals his father's intellectual and emotional invasions.

Sam invested many months in finding his own zipper on his inside (his internal locus of control). He found his voice and finally began to stand up to his father.

In Lucy's case, she saw how her father had crossed the generational line as well, which included physical violations. He would walk into her bathroom as though there were no need for personal space. When he sat on the couch, he would throw his arms around the back of the couch and take up enough room for at least two people. When teased about that behavior, he always attributed it to his coming from New York and laughed it off.

But not all boundary issues are intrusions; other boundary problems are from neglect, when little or no limit-setting occurs in a chaotic family system. All too often a lonely parent may cross that generational line, and the child does not realize that being Mom's or Dad's "chosen" one also leaves the child caught in a family triangle.

In families, a clear line must be drawn between the generations, but that does not mean that the line must be rigidly drawn. Ethnicity also plays an important role in how rigid the line is. People from Mediterranean countries are typically much more comfortable with close personal space and the use of touch when speaking to one another. Italian and Greek families, for example, are comfortable with close personal space as well as open expression of feelings. In contrast, many Scandinavians prefer a greater distance in their personal space. I often tease clients that they can determine what was allowed in their families by looking back at their mother's kitchen cupboards or pantries, suggesting that the degree to which there was olive oil was the degree to which they could experience emotional expressiveness.

Boundaries: The Zipper to the Self

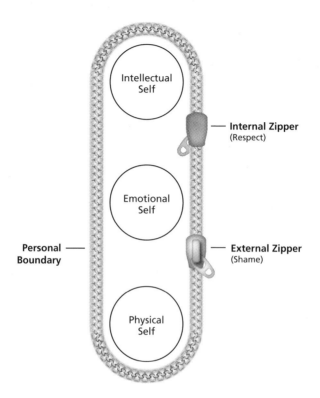

Leaders who develop clear, strong boundaries often do so because they want to make a difference in how they demonstrate leadership. To set clear, healthy boundaries, they had to learn not to be afraid of their shadows and to understand the difference between putting up fences around their past emotional lives and setting boundaries in how those emotions appropriately play out in their present work environment.

Moving Beyond Shame by Facing Vulnerability

For a leader to become genuine requires a willingness to face vulnerability. For shame-bound individuals, becoming vulnerable is most difficult. It means exposing who you really are, which is the core of genuine leadership. Brené Brown, nationally known author and researcher, cites three components of vulnerability: uncertainty, being at risk, and emotional exposure. The latter, facing emotional exposure, is difficult for those who grew up in shame-bound systems. In the work world particularly, a myth persists that vulnerability is weakness. The expression of feelings in the workplace has typically been seen as "touchy-feely," as "sappy," or as weakness. Brené Brown suggests otherwise. "If you are alive and in relationship, you do vulnerability," she tells us. "If you are alive and in relationship and in business, you do it hourly."[7]

This idea brings to my mind a coaching client named Steve. He had risked vulnerability at home and in his friendship circles by sharing childhood stories of his early wounds. Much of his healing came through journal writing. He declared, "I can never lie to my journal." He then began writing poetry. When he made the decision to retire early, he told me how his closing with the firm surprised him at first, but then became a valid learning experience. As his team members circled up to say their final farewells, Steve pulled a paper out of his pocket; it was a poem about his career and what might lie ahead. Of course, he had unwittingly broken the "don't be vulnerable" rule at work. He reported that the group all stared at him in silence. His immediate reaction and self-talk was, "I never should have done this; they don't 'get' it." By the time he went back to his cubicle and passed a mirror on the outer wall, he looked at himself and said, "You did the right thing, Self; you let them know you."

Vulnerability surely means risking, for there is no guarantee of a positive outcome, and the expression of feelings is indeed a starting point. When you gain the wisdom of vulnerability, however, it is also important to know with whom to *not* be vulnerable. You don't risk vulnerability if your gut tells you that you are not safe. It takes raw courage to reveal the hidden parts of yourself, and it is just one more step toward genuine leadership.

For many, learning vulnerability also involves a willingness to fail.

Downclimbing

Recently as a requirement for a leadership award nomination, I had to tell a story of what had most greatly affected my ability to lead. I was surprised at the story that leapt out: the story of my first downclimb.

I had been leading family climbing groups, a program that grew out of my work when teaching medical residents affective education at the University of Minnesota Medical School. Upon completion of the class's rock-climbing trip in the Black Hills of South Dakota, three of my climbing friends asked if I wanted to join them in a climb at Devils Tower in northern Wyoming. Devils Tower is a rock monolith rising 5,117 feet out of the talus and rubble. My friends reminded me that it would be the hardest climb I had ever done and that I had to commit to the climb. Without a pause, I had immediately replied, "Sure, I can commit to that."

We camped out in the rich Wyoming grasses, but I could not sleep. My friend's words repeatedly filled me: "There's no turning back, Marilyn, when you've committed to the climb." At 4 a.m. we began making our way up 300 feet of large boulders. When we stood at the base of the climb, I looked up at the tall rock spirals. My mouth became dry—"fear glue" I came to call it—as waves of fear overtook me. The first pitch of the climb was called the Leaning Column because of its resemblance to a broken ancient Grecian column. I heard the call from above: "On belay," signifying that my belayer, Rolf, who climbed before me and would serve as my anchor, was steady and ready for me to climb. Shaking, I tied the rope into my carabiners and adjusted my helmet. I knew enough not to stand frozen in fear but to move on. We had already double-checked my knots and done a complete safety check. Then my belayer called down, "Climb." Taking a deep breath, I closed my eyes for a few seconds and replied in a faked strong voice, "Climbing." For a while I moved steadily up the rock column, but ever so slowly. Suddenly I fell. "Falling," I cried. I found a stable foothold and felt Rolf tighten his hold on the rope. I breathed a sigh of relief; I knew I could trust my belayer. But I also realized I could never make it up six more "pitches" of the climb and get back down successfully. I had very little of the upper body strength required for this climb. By the time I reached the top of the column, I heaved my body over it to rest. I was totally exhausted and still filled with fear.

Rolf called down to me, "Marilyn, the next pitch is twice as hard." I gulped, realizing there was no way I could do the next pitch in this exhausted state. I looked up with tears running down my cheeks and called back, "Rolf, I need to be lowered," and he realized I could not complete the climb. Slowly, he released rope as I lowered myself down the rock face. Feelings flooded me—anger, shame, self-hatred—and self-talk of being too old, being a woman, being ill prepared, being too overweight. I had never faced such a flood of feelings in my life. They continued to bubble up. Then suddenly my right foot landed on one of the large rock boulders we had just climbed in the early dawn. I felt remarkable relief. My other foot planted. I said to myself, "Marilyn, you have just made one of the wisest decisions of your adult life."

It was hard for me to admit that I wasn't ready for the climb. I had always focused on being competent and prided myself on keeping commitments. I had not known failure intimately in my life. "Why now?" I asked myself. However, my body could not lie: I was not mentally, emotionally, or physically ready for that climb.

The sense of relief eclipsed the shameful feelings quickly; I prepared a fine picnic dinner that afternoon for the rest of our climbing group. I did, by the way, return the next year to climb again, but I did it just for me—to prove to myself and to no one else that I was prepared for my climb. But the learning from that first climb seared indelibly into my brain; my vulnerability had been forced upon me. For some of us, it takes a dramatic experience to learn true vulnerability.

This had been my first real downclimb in my life. Before then,

I had been very fortunate and successful in most of what I had attempted, but I learned far more from this single downclimb than any life "climb" I had ever successfully completed. The downclimb revealed my real self—my tearful, emotional self who took the risk of being exposed—and I had failed! I did not know how to handle failure. I don't think I have ever been so exposed since, but this downclimb truly set the path for my ongoing safety in exhibiting my vulnerability.

Pathways for Change

These exercises, including an autobiographical narrative and a disempowering and empowering behaviors assessment, provide useful tools for you to continue to explore the ideas from this chapter.

Autobiographical Narrative

Upon completion of the family genogram, try writing your true story of what shaped you as an authentic person and as a leader. Writing a personal narrative can be enhanced by what you learn from family interviews. The resulting "revisionist" story allows you to own who you are, with all your strengths and weaknesses. I often have to remind clients that "no one gets it all" (i.e., no family escapes the life events that shape us). We all have stories. What is essential is that we own our stories truthfully.

The first natural step toward igniting change in your business is to get an honest view of your family dynamics. Change is indeed possible by taking the journey home.

Disempowering and Empowering Behaviors Assessment

Focus first on your shadows, or disempowering behaviors. On the chart on page 51, rank yourself on each Disempowering Behavior using the rating scale of 1 for Never/Seldom to 5 for Almost Always. If you're uncertain of what each behavior might entail, consult the list of examples of disempowering behaviors that accompanies the chart. When you have finished, add up the numbers you've circled for disempowering behaviors. The maximum score can be 105, but the lower your number, the better chances you have as a change agent. A perfect score, indicating you very seldom engage in disempowering behaviors, would be 21—but if this is your score, double-check your honesty scale or your denial pattern! None of us is perfect; this instrument is to help you identify behaviors that sabotage real cultural change. If you find yourself in the range over 75, you might want to hire a coach.

Now focus on your strengths, or empowering behaviors. On the chart on page 52, rank yourself on each Empowering Behavior using the rating scale of 1 for Never/Seldom to 5 for Almost Always. When you have finished, add up the numbers you've circled for empowering behaviors. If you have a perfect score of 105, you probably also have high emotional intelligence and can help in creating a dynamic, robust work system.

Examples of Disempowering Behaviors

If you feel uncertain of what a disempowering behavior might involve, consult this list to help you complete the assessment.

1. Rejecting, attacking, countering

   - Rejecting or putting down others' ideas.

   - Countering, saying no to everything, constantly playing devil's advocate.

   - Monday morning quarterbacking.

   - Doubting, questioning, making it hard for others to feel safe.

   - "I know you worked hard on this, but there just has to be another way to do it."

2. Making fun of others

   - Using sarcasm, zingers.

   - Joking with double-edged humor.

   - Gossiping, telling stories about others' mistakes.

   - Making open put-downs with fake laughter ("You really thought they would accept that proposal in that form?").

3. Withholding

   - Being stingy with information, keeping information close to the chest.

   - Stuffing feelings, not sharing personal feelings, and denying those of others.

- Giving misinformation, not committing or revealing positions.
- Doing things on your own and not informing others, not letting others influence you.
- "I was sure that Sam sent you the new safety regulations."
- Holding secrets.

4. Distracting, pretending, fogging

- Pretending everything is all right, masking feelings.
- Changing subjects, jumping the track.
- Keeping people off balance with hidden agendas, asking questions instead of making statements.
- Avoiding through complimenting or jamming agendas.
- "Do you think you want to have that meeting next Wednesday?" (meaning "I want us to meet next Wednesday").

5. Dismissing, discounting, disqualifying

- Ignoring someone, giving other projects higher priority.
- Proposing unrealistic schedules and timelines.
- Discounting, implying "You don't count," "That's not important," or "It can't change."
- Voicing pessimism and deep concerns and fears.
- Rendering someone invisible through excluding that person or their contributions.
- "Oh, I didn't realize we had scheduled that team meeting for today."
- Not speaking up, passivity, indicating "I don't count."

6. Blaming, punishing

- "Getting even," carrying grudges ("Don't get mad; get even"), spreading gossip.

- Blaming someone else, berating others—or blaming your-self, playing martyr.
- Not accepting responsibility—or accepting all responsibility.
- "Shoulding" and "oughting" someone.
- "I'm sorry, but you should have let me know you were in-terested in that promotion I gave to Joe. Why didn't you tell me?"

7. Controlling
- Exhibiting "power over" interaction.
- Domineering, demanding, giving orders.
- Manipulating others, carrying secrets.
- Controlling information, dedicating inadequate resources and/or training.
- Using helplessness or ignorance to "hold" others.
- "You know these reports are to be completed each week."

8. Sabotaging
- Intentional malicious disobedience, knowingly doing the wrong thing to make a boss or coworker look bad or doing so through giving misinformation.
- Stealing someone's ideas, claiming them for your own, hurt-ing others.
- Not alerting others to information you have.
- After supporting a project, launching in a new direction—without telling others.
- Telling your boss something about another behind that person's back.
- "But when I called the meeting and told you what was needed, I assumed you would take charge of all of it."

9. Criticizing

- Finding flaws, looking for what is wrong.
- Verbally or nonverbally disapproving, not rewarding or recognizing efforts.
- Judging, only one set of standards, correcting others.
- Asking questions with sharp edges.
- "Here we go again—another system to get excited about."

10. Intimidating

- Making yourself seem powerful, either nonverbally or verbally.
- Serving self-interests, owning the expert status.
- Bullying, demanding, talking "down" to people.
- Arriving late, acting with privilege.
- "Are you ready for my evaluation of your program?" (spoken in a haughty tone).

11. Trivializing

- Leaving someone's meeting agenda item for last.
- Implying that an accomplishment was just okay, having low expectations.
- Suggesting that anyone could have done it (whatever it was).
- Not acknowledging someone's contributions, which may also be shown in salary or title.
- "Well, I know it's important to you, but our budget just can't include it this year; be patient."

12. Excusing

- Not expecting much of a particular race or gender.
- Making excuses for people's behavior, explaining it away.
- Maintaining low expectations of coworkers, low morale.

- Being overly sympathetic.
- "Well, I know Jack would have met the deadline if he had had better instructions."

13. Name calling, labeling
    - Teasing through name calling.
    - Identifying people through their faults (for example, calling someone "the latecomer").
    - Making mean-spirited put-downs of coworkers or bosses.
    - Talking behind people's backs, eroding confidence in them.
    - "You jerk—you never get it straight."

14. Forgetting
    - Not taking responsibility.
    - Forgetting people's names.
    - Procrastinating.
    - Trying to hold information in your head.
    - "I had no idea you wanted to have that done by Tuesday of this week!"

15. Denying
    - Denying some event or behavior occurred, intentionally forgetting.
    - Not commenting on inappropriate behaviors.
    - Not acknowledging feelings.
    - Not owning personal responsibility.
    - "That never did happen" or "I never told you that."

16. Distrusting
    - Acting suspicious.
    - Speaking with cynicism.
    - Questioning in a doubting tone.

- Being overly responsible—only you can get it done.
- "Are you certain that you have all the preparations set for the meeting?"

17. Intruding

- Completing others' sentences (which is often fogged as being helpful).
- Entering offices without knocking, interrupting.
- Prying, probing questioning.
- "Triangling" into others' conversations (joining them, uninvited, to add your opinion), or "I heard Sue say . . ."
- Interrupting with "Oh, which reminds me of a time when I . . ."

18. Egotism, selfishness

- Hurting others to advance oneself.
- Not acknowledging others' needs.
- Making sure that your self-interest is always served.
- Changing, controlling agendas to promote yourself.
- "Well, I did it because management has known I do this better than anyone."

19. Competing, perfectionism

- Wearing the "white" hat, being "special."
- Flattering high-status people, namedropping.
- Being politically ambitious, "working" people to gain attention.
- Pridefully taking credit, not giving others credit.
- Making side deals with coworkers.
- "Yep, it felt good to learn I was the one asked to supervise this project."

20. Reacting

- Expressing knee-jerk responses to certain people, to certain words.
- Not controlling emotions, responding with charged feelings.
- Leaving—whether psychologically or physically.
- Retreating without commenting.
- "I never did tell you that!" or "You always try to say it's me!"

21. Abusing

- Criticizing workers in front of others, being disrespectful.
- Assaulting others with anger.
- Exhibiting aggressive behavior, pounding on a table, yelling.
- Talking in hostile, sarcastic tones.
- Taking revenge, holding on to grudges.
- "Look, Jones, just why in hell couldn't you get this out on time?"

Disempowering Behaviors Assessment

	Never/Seldom				Almost Always
1. Rejecting, attacking, countering	1	2	3	4	5
2. Making fun of others	1	2	3	4	5
3. Withholding	1	2	3	4	5
4. Distracting, pretending, fogging	1	2	3	4	5
5. Dismissing, discounting, disqualifying	1	2	3	4	5
6. Blaming, punishing	1	2	3	4	5
7. Controlling	1	2	3	4	5
8. Sabotaging	1	2	3	4	5
9. Criticizing	1	2	3	4	5
10. Intimidating	1	2	3	4	5
11. Trivializing	1	2	3	4	5
12. Excusing	1	2	3	4	5
13. Name calling, labeling	1	2	3	4	5
14. Forgetting	1	2	3	4	5
15. Denying	1	2	3	4	5
16. Distrusting	1	2	3	4	5
17. Intruding	1	2	3	4	5
18. Egotism, selfishness	1	2	3	4	5
19. Competing, perfectionism	1	2	3	4	5
20. Reacting	1	2	3	4	5
21. Abusing	1	2	3	4	5

Empowering Behaviors Assessment

	Never/Seldom			Almost Always	
1. Contributing, adding to, accepting, asking fair questions	1	2	3	4	5
2. Empowering humor, lightness	1	2	3	4	5
3. Sharing, candor, openness, truthfulness, fairness	1	2	3	4	5
4. Inviting and paying real attention	1	2	3	4	5
5. Honoring, respecting, uplifting	1	2	3	4	5
6. Making "I" statements, taking responsibility	1	2	3	4	5
7. Requesting, sharing, giving	1	2	3	4	5
8. Honesty in all moves; supporting, bolstering	1	2	3	4	5
9. Seeking strengths, coaching, inspiring, being kind, suggesting, forgiving	1	2	3	4	5
10. Trusting, providing safe haven, treating all equally	1	2	3	4	5
11. Appreciating	1	2	3	4	5
12. Holding people accountable	1	2	3	4	5
13. Positive references and names	1	2	3	4	5
14. Remembering	1	2	3	4	5
15. Acknowledging reality and feelings	1	2	3	4	5
16. Asking for further clarification	1	2	3	4	5
17. Reading cues, politely waiting or asking permission	1	2	3	4	5
18. Sharing and caring	1	2	3	4	5
19. Listening for others' ideas, admitting mistakes	1	2	3	4	5
20. Reflecting, thinking before reacting	1	2	3	4	5
21. Appropriately expressing feelings, peacemaking	1	2	3	4	5

3

Leading Change

[LEADERSHIP STYLES]

*"If your actions inspire others to dream more, learn more,
do more, and become more, you are a leader."*

— JOHN QUINCY ADAMS, SIXTH PRESIDENT OF THE UNITED STATES

In the introduction, I mentioned the landmark Leadership IQ study showing that 46 percent of all newly hired CEOs fail within the first eighteen months.[1] Many current studies report findings as high as 67 percent! A failed executive costs an organization at every level— millions of dollars in entering and exiting fees, anxiety and cynicism in the organization, mistrust of leadership, and public skepticism about its corporate image. These dramatic shifts naturally affect company morale, but they also affect the shareholder confidence so important to most companies' financial success.

Despite the stories of tyrannical leaders—such as "Chainsaw" Al Dunlap, who headed both Scott Paper Co. and Sunbeam-Oster Co., only believed in short-term goals, and said, "If you want a friend, get a dog"—the failed-leadership syndrome continues. (Of the eight companies Dunlap headed, six no longer exist.) Perhaps we so frequently see failed leadership because people still cling to the myths of leadership, including these four:

Myth 1: Everyone can be a leader.

Not true. Many people in leadership roles don't have the self-knowledge or the authenticity necessary for leadership. That's why the problems in organizations are often caused by the leaders at the top.

Myth 2: People who get to the top are leaders.
Not necessarily. Many who make it to the top get there by their political acumen, not because of their leadership qualities.

Myth 3: Women are not effective leaders.
The reality is that their access to power is blocked. Many of the fastest-growing companies in America are led by women.

Myth 4: Change causes stress.
The fact is that preserving homeostasis of the system has higher costs.

One of the first questions I often ask clients came from the title of a September 2000 article in the *Harvard Business Review*: "Why Should Anyone Be Led by You?"[2] I was struck by the way my mentor, Carl Whitaker, phrased the idea this way: "You can teach what it is, you can teach how to do it, but you can never teach how to 'be' it." Most leadership development programs have focused on what leadership is and what leaders do, but little attention has been paid to what it means to *be* a leader. In executive development work, we have found that many leaders are eager to learn about *being* a leader, including how they present themselves and who they are to the world around them.

In 1996, Warren Bennis was referred to in *Forbes* magazine as "the dean of leadership gurus," a title that lasted for many years. Bennis, the author of the still best-selling book *On Becoming a Leader,* believes that leaders are not born, but made.[3] He stated, "The process of becoming a leader is, if not identical, certainly similar to the process of becoming a fully integrated human being. It's got to do with authenticity."

As we approach fresh perspectives on leadership, those who lead from authenticity will emerge as this century's leaders. The ability to know oneself, to use intuition, to be fully present, and to communicate integrity will determine who leads.

Leaders who can shine a light into their shadows are taking an essential step toward authenticity and, in doing so, can greatly affect their organization's culture and create a revived, often transformed, work culture. Of course, for such leaders to be successful, their companies' boards of directors must be supportive, for they hold the top power.

Often outside consultants are brought in to be the "hit men" and "hit women" when the board does not want to act upon certain issues in the head offices. For example, when a company CEO revealed to the board of directors that she was in love with one of the executive team members, the board did not act. The result was internal havoc, mistrust, and eroding relationships for many years. I saw another example of this, but with opposite results, when consulting for one of our national athletic leagues. Initially these famous coaches had turned their backs on their famous players' drug use and sexual exploitation. But eventually, the upper management and coaches joined together to take action. The results were improved performance with a positive impact on profits.

Awareness at the very top is needed to begin the movement of cultural change:

- leaders who are willing to be open to feedback and input from their employees and peers

- leaders who are mature enough not to expect perfection or to overreact to mistakes or problems

- leaders who are guided by the principles of tolerance, empathy, and acceptance

Leaders who possess these abilities can govern healthy, humane work environments.

Understanding Leadership Styles

Recognizing and understanding the advantages and disadvantages of different leadership styles and determining what style is a good fit for you can be a first step. This is a common practice for those seeking true transformation in their leadership. Most of us have become familiar to some degree with some of the standard positive "visionary," "coaching," "affiliative," and "democratic" styles introduced by Daniel Goleman in *Primal Leadership*.[4] These surely are approaches that many leaders strive to adopt, no matter what their principal style may be. Actually it's often *after* an interim "turn-around" leader or corporate renewal professional has come into a failing business with fresh perspective, objectivity, and the singular goal of turning the company around by making dramatic changes that many of the thoughtful, flexible leaders are put in place.

Jim Collins, a renowned management consultant who with Morten Hansen coauthored *Great by Choice*,[5] states, "The great leaders I've studied are all about people whose energy and drive are directed outward. It's not about themselves; it's about something greater than themselves." Collins has his own ways of looking at a leader; he lists thirteen leader archetypes. Two of the first three he mentions we've talked about in this book: emotionally intelligent and authentic.

I agree with Jim's assessment of great leaders being outward driven—and I would add that these leaders have likely searched inside and faced their shadows first so that they can then project outward. While it is true that there are some truly pathological leaders, I believe that failed leadership is born from those who are basically decent and competent but who have not faced their own shadows in their life stories. Today we read almost daily about the aggressive pursuit of profit and power. Many business writers have said these behaviors occur because of a lack of ethics training at leading business schools and law schools. One study showed that 56 percent of graduate business students admitted to cheating at least once in the academic year compared with 47 percent of students in other graduate programs.[6] And studies at the Harvard and Duke business schools revealed that MBA students who cheat typically lie to themselves, revealing a lack of personal awareness and insight into what motivates their behavior. This is, of course, what we often see played out in the leadership roles and executive suites across the country. Unresolved family issues can wear many masks in failed leadership. In exploring leadership styles of those with emotional baggage from their first family, I originally identified five broad categories of leadership styles. They are the Obsessive Perfectionist, the Narcissist, the Conflict Avoider, the Tyrant, and the Nice Guy. Recently I added a sixth category: the Introvert, also called the Reflective Leader.

The Obsessive Perfectionist

Perfectionists deny the role that shame has played in their lives. Under the false self of the perfectionist lies deep inadequacy, fear of failure, low emotional intelligence quotient, lack of empathy, and lack of self-trust. Perfectionistic shame-bound leaders fear making a mistake because they feel they *are* a mistake! Often the obsession seen in their rigidity and control is covered with a veneer of politeness. At an extreme, we can see the mask of "commanding" or abrasive leaders, who think they know best and want others to follow their ideas and strategies to the letter. ("I'll shame you before you can shame me!") So fearful of making mistakes, perfectionists become obsessive. Shame and fear of vulnerability go together in driving their obsession with perfection. As perfectionistic leaders face their buried fears and family stories, they can learn resilience. Leadership writer and a Ross School of Business professor at the University of Michigan, Noel Tichy wrote, "If I don't know your story, I don't know a thing about you as a leader."[7] When leaders can be open and vulnerable, they are able to talk about the pressures of their responsibilities, come to terms with their fear of failure, and become open to other ideas and the support of their peers and staff.

Bob was a keen example of someone I have often met in the business and organizational world. Unable to ask for change for himself, he approached his executive team (I believe unconsciously) to work on *their* "personal development in leadership." When I began working with Bob, I observed how, while he was effective in many ways, he also fit the typical model of obsessive perfectionism, using highly controlling leadership.

Through exploring his family history, exposing the secrets in the family shadows, Bob discovered how fear-driven he was. He realized that his compulsive work behaviors were linked to his fear that his family would "fall apart," as it had after his mother's long illness that ended in her death when Bob was six. Bob had learned to work compulsively to avoid any feelings—going all the way back to his childhood and his grief for his mother. His father's message had been "Be a man now; we will just carry on."

Young Bob had intuitively sensed his father's unexpressed grief and went on to be an achiever in all that he did, so his father would never worry about him. When Bob entered Wall Street, he found his "family" of compulsive workers doing what they called the "Japanese shift"—regularly working through the night. Bob was emotionally "safe" in this environment and very successful, rewarded well for his compulsive work habits—all considered normal there.

The financial rewards were high, but the personal costs even higher. At the time of our initial interviews, Bob's wife was talking about divorce and his children were estranged from him. He had just learned that he was going to be a grandfather but his daughter had not told him, thinking he would not come for the delivery. His family's feelings and attitudes were the result of his persistently allowing work to take precedence over everything else in his life. Bob painfully recalled that, in his drive for success, he had even missed his children's college graduations.

In follow-up coaching sessions, Bob was able to find out who he was and how he got there. He became aware of how the coping skills he had learned early in life were governing his decisions today. He also realized what the late Harry Levinson, a psychologist who was a pioneer in discovering the link between job conditions and emotional health, often said: "There is no change without loss."[8] Bob had never grieved his childhood losses. He acknowledged the frightened child in his past and began to share his painful stories with his wife and children. As he grew in self-awareness, Bob grew increasingly excited about the changes he was making personally and the connections he was feeling toward his family and his colleagues. As the CEO of his company, he knew that to bring his epiphanies into the workplace he would have to break many of his own rules. He also realized how many unconsciously and loyally followed rules had to be broken to create a workplace in which there was human development as well as economic growth.

Bob learned that not only most of the management team but also probably many of his direct reports had also normalized behaviors that were born out of the wounds of their past hidden in the shadows. As a result, he instituted new insurance plans that provided generous packages for family insurance coverage, including mental health policies for spouses and dependents of employees. "I never realized how important it is to get this stuff clear," he said. "Family help should be made available to everyone! What a difference it makes, and what a difference it can make at work. How could I not have seen this?" He asked this aloud, although he was now fully aware of the answer.

Bob's colleagues, with few exceptions, had seemed as oblivious as Bob had been to how the stories of their pasts, with the inherited beliefs, values, and attitudes, were playing out daily in their company. At first, people were suspicious of Bob's change in senior-management meetings when he asked for a brief personal "check-in" around the table. Soon they came to embrace the new process. Bob now received praise not only for the financial profits brought to the company but also for how he conducted meetings and for the attention he paid to the personal lives of his senior staff. He received notes of appreciation from family members and was honored at the annual sales meeting for the leadership he demonstrated. One of the new behaviors his colleagues noted was his ability to schmooze—his capacity to take a sincere interest in others.

Eventually, cautiously, Bob took his new approach even further. He developed his own "personal board of directors," a group of colleagues from other firms who met twice monthly to share their professional and personal concerns.

The Narcissist

The term *narcissist* typically is used in derogatory ways. However, many self-centered yet visionary leaders, such as successful financier George Soros, may be described as having positive narcissism. And a *Harvard Business Review* article tells the story of an Oracle executive who described the narcissistic former CEO Larry Ellison this way: "The difference between God and Larry is that God does not believe he is Larry."[9] Psychoanalyst Michael Maccoby explains that productive narcissists "attract followers with their compelling visions."[10] These leaders emerge to inspire people and to shape the future. Narcissism born out of shame, by contrast, wears a dark side—emotionally isolated, highly distrustful, highly image-conscious, and unable to connect with others. Many consultants have seen the "shadowed" narcissist as a person with a high degree of shame. These leaders resist any critical feedback whatsoever.

I knew I faced a challenge when meeting with Joyce, a hard-driving, high-profile, successful CEO. She had brought me in to gather feedback from her senior team. I was careful to report the interviews verbatim and in writing for her, so we could review them together. It did not matter that I approached her with sensitivity, understanding, and empathy; she immediately flew into a rage as she skimmed the first page. It was all I could do to remain seated and attempt to stay composed while she screamed, ranted, and raved that the comments must all be lies. I personally felt threatened. So this is what is meant by "narcissistic rage," I thought to myself. I recognized at that moment that this behavior required therapy, not coaching.

Narcissistic leaders fear vulnerability, which makes coaching a challenge of the highest order—some would say futile. A powerful woman, Joyce turned to her close circle of friends who supported her perception that it was about "them" and not her. The system stayed the same; she did not choose to take the journey home. And although she has been successful in business, many people now say, "Admire her from afar."

Many narcissistic leaders are seen as powerful. Their strong sense of self and their often extroverted, confident personalities intimidate many people who would describe them as power brokers. But everyone who is self-confident and competent isn't necessarily narcissistic, and a person doesn't have to be a power broker to seem intimidating to someone with low self-esteem or self-confidence issues.

I recall an experience I had some years ago when speaking at a business conference. Poet and business consultant David Whyte, the author of the best-selling book *The Heart Aroused: Poetry and the Preservation of the Soul in Corporate America,* presented just before I did.[11] I felt confident about my material, my talk, and my professional status. Yet when David finished speaking in his soothing, rich, English accent, I felt intimidated. What a surprise!

It was not at all that David was intimidating; it was just that I was so impressed with his presentation that I felt "lesser than." His poetry, his genuineness, and his speaking style were eloquent; he received a standing ovation. And it was well deserved. As I later reflected, what I had experienced was a glitch in my own self-confidence and a sense of humility, but he did not intimidate anyone. Certainly no one could classify him as a narcissistic or intimidating leader—but my story does illustrate that narcissism and intimidation can be relative.

The Conflict Avoider

To please all, conflict avoiders accommodate people so they can avoid conflict at any cost. Being liked is essential for these people. The result is that no one knows where the conflict avoider truly stands. They tend to avoid decision making, because if one avoids making decisions, conflict is avoided. Of course, so is progress! Although this mask can show a good "face," it often leads to the neglect of what these leaders know is needed for either themselves or the organization. Some of these leaders survive for a time because they hired strong direct reports who can be their "hit people." They typically are unaware of their own histories and are—under their veneer of cooperation—highly anxious. Their emotional dishonesty occurs not only with others but also with themselves.

Josh was the CEO of a publicly held corporation. He had also been serving on the firm's foundation board as an advisor. The foundation board consisted of several founding family members who were blindly loyal to their foundation's executive director (ED). When a new young family member, Tim, joined the board, he was shocked at what he saw. He had many questions about the board's structure and process. "How is it," he asked, "that you have been paying for your ED's around-the-world vacations?" There was immediate tension in the room, before someone replied, "Well, he has helped us all so much; it's the least we can do!" "But," Tim declared, "he is your employee; you *pay* him to work for you!" Tim proceeded to let the board members know the unethical aspect of their behavior, explaining that dual relationships are to be avoided. For many months, Tim was attacked by other family members. An outside consultant came in to help educate the board about boundaries and dual relationships. Outside the meeting room, Tim confronted Josh, asking how he could have allowed this to continue.

"Well, they really did see their executive director as their counselor, their friend, their children's confidant," Josh explained. Although he had long witnessed the executive director's abuse of power and privilege, Josh had never made a comment. Josh used the lame excuse that it really was "none of my business." Under his cover of accommodation, he was a cowardly leader, one who would not take risks at any price. Josh's family history is fairly predictable: He grew up as the codependent "family hero," the adult child in a highly perfectionistic, shame-bound family. He had learned to become overly responsible for the feelings and behaviors of others—to the exclusion of his own needs.

The Tyrant

An autocratic leader who creates an environment where he or she exercises complete authority and where resistance seems pointless is known as the tyrannical leader.

James was an outstanding chief operating officer (COO). His peers all recognized his strengths. However, James had modeled his leadership style after the company's tyrannical leader, Heinz. After some years with the firm, James had decided he wanted to put his name in the ring for succession to the CEO position. After receiving a 360-degree feedback report from his peers and the people who reported to him, James realized that he was seen as mean, bullying, sarcastic, and shaming in his leadership—a good working definition of the tyrannical leader. For more than three years now, he has been working on changing those behaviors. He learned through exploring his family history that his desire to be the favorite "son" of the CEO was identical to his wanting to be his dad's special child, a task he never could achieve. Now that he recognized his self-sabotage, he was engaged in coaching work to make real changes in his behaviors. A more recent 360-degree review revealed that people did indeed see his changes, but they also held on to old images of the raging James, the mean-spirited James. He felt caught. He had worked hard to make real changes; they were indeed real, as people had noticed and reported on his changed behavior. But he did not know how to handle his past.

With his coach's advice, he decided to go to each of the subgroups with whom he worked. He met with each group independently. He made amends. He told his story and asked for forgiveness, and he asked people to trust that his changes were there for the long haul. He also talked with the current CEO, Heinz, about what he was doing within the company. Since Heinz used the same intimidating behaviors and got away with them because of his role in the firm, he had been suspicious about James's changes. He now decided he would give James a chance, despite being aware that he was the model for James's earlier tyrannical leadership behavior. Finally, James became the top candidate for CEO and ultimately did get the position. James was grateful, for he knew that his self-sabotage might have eventually been the end of his career in the firm.

The Nice Guy

The Nice Guy leadership style refers to the leader who avoids confrontation, often adopting a "laissez-faire" style to avoid conflict. A nice guy leader is often seen as one who is smart and has heart, but may not show his or her spine. This leadership style is one of generosity, but often to a fault.

Andrew was being considered for promotion to executive vice president of his firm. The firm's president asked for coaching for Andrew. He had concerns about Andrew's being "too open, too available to too many people." The president added, "He is surely smart enough and liked by all, but we don't know if he will be able to do the job. His door is always open to too many of his team." In my initial interview with Andrew about his family history, I learned that he grew up in a small town in a family in which communication was quite closed. His parents had a cool, distant relationship. Andrew was often the center of any real (and really polite) conversation. He was musically talented, and his parents struggled financially to make it possible for him to go to a two-week "sleep-away" music camp. When Andrew returned, he discovered his mother had moved out; his parents were divorcing. The meaning Andrew took from this, at age eleven, was, "If I'm not here, things will fall apart."

Andrew and I were both amazed that this was the particular story he chose to tell me in our first meeting. How valuable it was for Andrew to learn the connection between his early meaning-making and his role at work. He had never considered that his pleasing, openness, and availability were linked to his childhood search for meaning and his need to be (overly) responsible for his family, both his original family and now his work family. It did not take Andrew long to change his behaviors, learn how to close his office door, and set limits for his meeting time with his direct reports. He managed his boundaries clearly and quickly. He knew the source for his behaviors, which made the changes much easier. And yes, he did get the job.

All five of these leadership styles—the Obsessive Perfectionist, Narcissist, Conflict Avoider, Tyrant, and Nice Guy—share a common thread of unethical behaviors. It would be simple for any of them to say, "You see, it wasn't my fault—it was that dysfunctional family I grew up in." We all have stories. It is up to each of us to understand our own leadership style. What better power center than the workplace, where we spend a high number of waking hours, to focus on personal growth?

You might remember I mentioned six leadership styles. This last style, the Introvert, or the Reflective Leader, emerges not so much from shadows as from inclination—and brings its own challenges to individuals, because this style defies a cultural myth.

The Introvert, or the Reflective Leader

One of our cultural myths is that great leaders are extroverts, but that simply does not prove to be true. Many studies reveal that the public sees extroverts as smarter, more attractive, and more likable. A Stanford Graduate School of Business study revealed that verbal fluency and sociability are the two most important predictors of success.[12]

Susan Cain wrote a best-selling book, *Quiet: The Power of Introverts in a World That Can't Stop Talking*,[13] in which she describes the power of the introverted leader. Cain points out that culturally we see talkers as more intelligent than the quieter types, despite the fact that myriad tests prove this to be inaccurate. When it comes to leadership, she states that we also see talkers as leaders, yet research shows no such link between loquaciousness and greater insight. In fact, Bradley Agle of Brigham Young University studied the CEOs of 128 major companies and discovered that leaders considered to be charismatic by their top executives had larger salaries but *not* better performance in their companies.[14] Management writer Jim Collins never intended to look at leadership, but when he searched for common threads in the highest performing companies, he found that he could not ignore the nature of the CEOs. All these companies were led by someone described by their employees and peers as *unassuming!* Collins found general agreement that they were perceived as "quiet, humble, modest, reserved, shy, gracious, mild-mannered, self-effacing, understated."[15]

Cain cites research showing that *one-third to one-half* of Americans are introverts. These are startling statistics to most of us who fail to recognize that many of our leaders are really introverts *acting* as extroverts! One place Cain researched was the Harvard Business School, a highly regarded producer of many of our country's great leaders. The school's entire curriculum focuses on extroversion—a person's ability to reek of self-confidence, to be gregarious and highly verbal. And yet consider these highly recognized names of introverted leaders: Abraham Lincoln, Warren Buffett, and Bill Gates.

Attitude Is Everything

Whether leaders are introverted or extroverted, one common denominator surpasses all others—and that is their attitude. Attitude can indeed be the "difference maker," as stated by John Maxwell, pastor turned leadership expert. I believe there's a degree to which we *choose* our attitudes.

The root word for *attitude* is *aptitude*, meaning "fitness." Maxwell writes, "You cannot disconnect attitude from reality and expect success."[16] In the introduction, I cited a Leadership IQ study that showed that 46 percent of all new hires would fail within eighteen months.[17] Other research by that global leadership training and research firm studied 5,247 hiring managers who collectively hired more than twenty thousand employees during the three-year study period. A startling discovery was that 89 percent of failed leaders (who left under pressure, were terminated, garnered negative performance reviews, and received disciplinary action) failed not for lack of technical skills, but for attitude!

The study found the following reasons why new hires fail:

- 26 percent because they can't accept feedback

- 23 percent because they're unable to understand and manage emotions

- 17 percent because they lack the necessary motivation to excel

- 15 percent because they have the wrong temperament for the job

- 11 percent because they lack the necessary technical skills[18]

Stated another way, the failed leaders were missing these traits:

- coachability (26 percent): the ability to accept and implement feedback from bosses, colleagues, and others

- emotional intelligence (23 percent): the ability to understand and manage one's emotions and accurately assess others' emotions

- motivation (17 percent): sufficient drive to achieve one's full potential and excel in the job

- temperament (15 percent): attitude and personality suited to the particular job and work environment

- technical competence (11 percent): functional or technical skills required to do the job[19]

Of the missing traits, only one, technical competence, didn't have to do directly or indirectly with attitude.

A key attitude trait often overlooked in hiring leaders is optimism. Psychologist Martin Seligman, author of *Learned Optimism: How to Change Your Mind and Your Life*,[20] emphasizes that most successful leaders are optimistic in their outlooks. The field of positive psychology has shown in recent years that a positive attitude can lead to success. This concept fits well with another important one—that the good leader is also a *learner*. Attitudes and behaviors are "learned," and thus can be unlearned and changed. In coaching businesspeople, I have found that when they learn to change their "self-talk," they begin to change their attitudes.

Attitude and Signs of Change

Signs of positive attitude supported by optimism were apparent when Cha Guzmán reported to work as the incoming president of Santa Fe Community College. When she arrived there, she was given a police escort to the large college campus. As she stepped out of her car, she saw a large faculty group awaiting her. They all wore sunglasses and held up placards that read, "We Need to Wear Sunglasses:

Our Future Is So Bright!" What an example of positive attitude—
and what a welcome to their new president!

Listening and Questioning

Besides an optimistic attitude, another key factor in successful leadership is one's ability to listen. Good listeners are attentive, focused,
and willing to engage fully.

Most researchers find that about 45 percent of our time in communication is spent in listening, but we only take in about half of
what we hear. It is alarming to note that, by extension, we can posit
that most leaders are poor listeners. A compilation of four studies
showed that the higher up people were in the organizational power
ladder, the less likely they were to accept advice because of their own
inflated self-confidence. That research, from the Queendom testing
company, reveals these statistics:

- 17 percent of listeners have a tendency to interrupt
- 19 percent will purposely divert or end conversations that
  don't interest them
- 27 percent make disapproving faces if they don't agree with
  the speaker
- 31 percent are thinking about how they will respond to the
  speaker
- 40 percent admit their mind wanders if they find the topic
  of conversation boring[21]

In coaching leadership teams, I often demonstrate three kinds of
listening:

- take-away listening to gain advantage
- directive listening to convince
- engaged listening to discover

(You'll find examples of all three kinds in Pathways for Change at
the end of this chapter.)

After I demonstrate these three listening styles, the leadership team members divide into pairs to practice one type, engaged listening. Unlike take-away or directive listening, engaged listening is essential to developing emotional intelligence—empathizing with the feelings of others. Engaged listening builds relationships as people seek understanding, trust is established, empathy is felt, and a context of partnership is created. The goal is connection. Participants find that their listening can be improved when they are aware of their own listening skills. When there is conflict among team members, a genuine leader often will ask the "contenders" to sit facing one another and engage in the very simple and effective practice of speaking truthfully and listening.

To illustrate, once when I was working with the leadership team in a family business, I could sense the tensions in the room at the start of our retreat. This Scandinavian family was very polite, very reserved. The family members often hid their feelings. If asked if something was wrong, they typically would respond, "Everything is fine."

Recognizing the power of the father, who was founder of their business, I asked him to demonstrate with me the three types of listening, using a story from their real lives. When we went to the front of the room, he began by saying that he was not sure what kind of twenty-fifth anniversary the company should celebrate, especially in a down-turned economy. I immediately demonstrated take-away listening by interrupting him, telling him that he reminded me of a time when I had a similar problem. Then I asked the group to comment on what they saw and heard—their father stepping back, the immediate surprised look on his face, and such. The group could clearly identify take-away listening; the family commented on the rudeness of the interruption, how the conversation became about me and not him.

Then I asked him to continue with his story. Giving him a little more time, but not much, I interrupted him again, this time giving him advice as to what I thought he should do: "You know, you really ought to make this what you want . . . ." I was using directive listening. Again, the rest of the family commented on how I only heard what I needed to convince him of my point of view. They also noted my nonverbal action—stepping closer into his personal space.

After everyone in the group commented, I asked their dad to continue once more. This time I practiced engaged listening, inquiring about what he thought his options were, empathizing about how tough it must be for him in his position to want to do something grand in a down-turned economy. The group noted the change of tone in my voice, as well as in their dad's voice, our mutual eye contact, the dialogue that we had created, my empathic responses to his dilemma, and their dad's newly expressed vulnerability, because when he was feeling heard, he could let his real feelings of disappointment be heard.

After this encounter, the rest of the family members were eager to have their own turns in facing one another to discuss difficult issues. By the day's end, there was a definite change in the room. The group began to laugh, to tease, to relax with one another. They said that, for the first time, they had felt heard.

Although listening is key to effective leadership, another dimension is also relevant—questioning. Gary Cohen is an executive coach and founder of CO2 Partners. In his book *Just Ask Leadership: Why Great Managers* Always *Ask the Right Questions,* Cohen focuses on the high percentages of top leaders who don't just tell, but ask.[22] Gary's creative approach fits clearly with ideas of the late Peter Drucker, a leading management consultant and self-proclaimed "social ecologist," who proposed the theory that "The leader of the past was a person who knew how to tell. The leader of the future will be a person who knows how to ask."

I recall a remarkable meeting I attended several years ago. My clients were going to conduct their annual "review" of *their* clients. They had invited representatives of about eight of their major customers to attend this special meeting held in a local hotel. Their customers sat on one side of the table; the senior executive team sat directly across from them. The customers began by asking a list of questions they had chosen together regarding my clients' service, their timeliness, their quality. The room was filled with leaders; the customers knew they had the power of remaining customers or moving on to a competitor. The dialogue began; the customers were candid, expressing their concerns, their satisfactions, their desires moving forward. I had never experienced such an honest, forthright conversation that indeed resulted in a win-win outcome. My clients were able to say what was possible and what was not possible, and with the "impossibles," they provided solid reasons. They were going to remain true to their mission and would not lower their standards. This, to me, was a great example of "just ask" leadership.

I think it is difficult to apply just one descriptor to a leader. Often we are blends of several traits; after all, we are human. Among even the most genuine of us, our attitude may not include the same degree of optimism every day, and some days we listen and question better than other days. Workers at all levels, no matter what type of leadership style their employer follows, have learned to adapt to these variations in their bosses and coworkers. They know the importance of emotional intelligence, a topic introduced earlier. Let's look more in depth at emotional intelligence as a leadership trait.

Emotional Intelligence

Dan Goleman, the psychologist and author of several books on emotional intelligence, is considered the leader of ethics and behavior in the workplace. In his research at nearly two hundred global companies, he found that, although leadership qualities that we typically see, such as cognitive intelligence, toughness, determination, and vision, are required for success, they are insufficient.[23]

Truly effective leaders are also distinguished by a high degree of emotional intelligence, which includes self-awareness, self-regulation, motivation, empathy, and social skills.

When Goleman analyzed competency models from 188 companies to determine which personal capabilities drove outstanding performance within these organizations and to what degree they did so, he found dramatic results. Although intellect was a driver of outstanding performance, as were cognitive skills and long-term vision, "emotional intelligence proved to be twice as important as the others for jobs at all levels."[24]

Goleman said in an online interview with another emotional intelligence expert, Joshua Freedman, that today's all-too-common lapses in ethics call for a new emphasis on leadership.[25] What is needed, he said, are these types of leaders:

- Leaders who are trustworthy. They walk their talk. He points out that trust takes time to build and also to rebuild.

- Leaders who will help us be secure and safe—an archetypal role. Leaders who will be available to turn to when we're in trouble.

In echoing the words of other leaders today, Goleman said that service aspects, not shareholder value, will grow more ethically sound practices. Joshua Freedman has pointed out that our culture is deeply entrenched in short-term profit. Both have said that leaders who survive long-term are trustworthy. But Goleman pointed out that what is crucial to improved leadership is the role of self-awareness as a leader. Goleman emphasizes in his recent writings that how we lead is how we know ourselves.[26]

Bruce Clarke, CEO of CAI, a human resources management firm, wrote in "The View from HR," his column on NewsObserver.com: "People are emotional first and rational second: Logic makes people think; emotions make people act."[27]

According to an article by Persis Swift on CAI's "Workplace Insights" blog,[28] Clarke believes that business leaders with strong emotional intelligence are more successful in hiring, managing growth, leading people, and teaching others. He offers four tips to improve emotional intelligence quotient, or EQ:

1. Analyze yourself and take responsibility for all your actions.

2. Really listen. Ask clarifying questions as needed.

3. Be aware of body language. Watch for facial expressions, tone of voice, and body and eye movements.

4. Identify what causes you stress. Recognize that you alone hold the power to bring yourself back to a calm state of mind.

By exploring the leadership types listed earlier, along with the how-tos of emotional intelligence, I think we can agree with the influential Frances Hesselbein, founder of the Leader to Leader Institute, who teaches that leadership begins *not* with what you do but with who you are. And an essential part of knowing who we are is the courage and ability to tell our stories as fully and honestly as possible, thereby bringing our shadows into the light.

Pathways for Change

The following exercises include a leadership traits questionnaire, suggestions for forming your own personal board of directors, a measurement of your optimism, examples of the three listening styles, and an emotional intelligence assessment. Together, they provide useful tools for you to continue to explore the ideas from this chapter.

Leadership Traits Questionnaire

Please rank yourself on the following positive leadership traits using the following values:

Strongly Disagree–0; Disagree–1; Slightly Disagree–2; Slightly Agree–3; Agree–4; Strongly Agree–5

Self-Awareness	Low					High
I use intuition.	0	1	2	3	4	5
I feel self-trust.	0	1	2	3	4	5
I am aware of my values.	0	1	2	3	4	5
My ego is intact.	0	1	2	3	4	5
I am aware of my purpose in life.	0	1	2	3	4	5

Self-Regulation						
I have good mood regulation.	0	1	2	3	4	5
I can suspend judgment in order to understand.	0	1	2	3	4	5
I can manage my reactivity.	0	1	2	3	4	5
I take critical feedback well.	0	1	2	3	4	5
I am comfortable with ambiguity.	0	1	2	3	4	5
I can laugh at myself.	0	1	2	3	4	5

Empathy

I am sensitive to the feelings of others.	0	1	2	3	4	5
I am a good listener.	0	1	2	3	4	5
I hear feedback from others about my empathy.	0	1	2	3	4	5
I can understand the emotional makeup of others.	0	1	2	3	4	5

Followership

I can develop a "we" culture.	0	1	2	3	4	5
I am able to delegate without micromanaging.	0	1	2	3	4	5
I have a good sense of humor as a leader.	0	1	2	3	4	5

This scoring can be used either individually or compiled as a group or team profile. This list can be helpful in a checklist for self-awareness improvement. Tally your scores and interpret the results below.

78–90: You've got it; keep practicing.
65–77: Identify growth areas.
0–64: Seek further personal growth work.

Personal Board of Directors

One of the key, and often unspoken, issues for leaders is the loneliness they experience. Typically, they cannot turn to subordinates or even their executive team for support with the loneliness they experience in their decision making. Here is where the *personal* board of directors comes in. The term *board of directors* evokes thoughts of long conference-room tables lined with executives deliberating weighty matters of corporate governance. But the board of directors model can also be a personal resource. While research shows deep friendships have health benefits and ease stress, some leaders go a step further and rely on close friends or family members as a kind of personal board of directors. Just like a corporate board, these allies serve (we hope!) as an honest, confidential sounding board for making tough career, family, and financial decisions.

Think of people in your life with diverse personalities and talents whom you might ask to be on your personal board of directors. Write down their names and then write what each one will bring to the group. You may be calling upon them as a group or in individual communication.

Learned Optimism

One of the finest instruments available online is the Learned Optimism Test on the Stanford University website. This 48-item test (which takes about 15 minutes) will measure your optimism. It includes ratings on self-esteem, pessimism, hope, and optimism. Go to http://www.stanford.edu/class/msande271/onlinetools/LearnedOpt .html to find the test.

For the Learned Optimism Test scoring, go to www.psychology .ccsu.edu/engwall/optimism.ppt. To use the results, look for online webinars and read Martin Seligman's book *Learned Optimism: How to Change Your Mind and Your Life.*[29]

Examples of Three Styles of Listening

Write down or record examples of the three styles of listening in conversations in your workplace. Use these examples to increase awareness of listening skills and leadership.

Take-Away Listening to Gain Advantage, or "It's Really about Me!"
This type of listening is all about having power.

- Wanting to lead, to persuade.

- "I know what is best."

- "Don't you think that you really ought to . . . ?"

Directive Listening to Convince and Clarify, or "I Want to Know . . . ."
In directive listening, the point is to control the speaker or the situation.

- Leading questions, such as "Don't you think . . . ?"

- Closed questions, to which the response can only be yes or no.

- Multiple questions (one after another).

- "Why?" questions.

Respectful or Engaged Listening to Learn, Discover

Those truly *engaged* in listening demonstrate mutual respect.

- "What?" "Where?" and "When?" questions (no "Why?" questions)

- Clarifying.

- Empathizing.

- Summarizing.

Emotional Intelligence

Queendom's Emotional Intelligence Test (www.queendom.com) is an online assessment tool that identifies your emotional intelligence personality type. As with the enneagram, people have found comfort in recognizing that their own emotional intelligence contributes to the interpersonal struggles they face and create. In short, while we bring our inherited family patterns to work, we also bring our unique personalities.

While this test is helpful for individuals, it is also useful with groups or teams where results are shared. It invites participation, vulnerability, and initial stages of practicing emotional intelligence. Readers will get a list of strengths and areas needing work. You can also receive detailed interpretation and advice. These shared results have strengthened many teams and leadership groups.

4

In a Different Voice

[WOMEN LEADING]

"You must do the thing you think you cannot do."

— ELEANOR ROOSEVELT, FIRST LADY OF THE UNITED STATES (1933–1945),
CREDITED WITH BROADENING THE ROLE OF THE PRESIDENT'S WIFE
TO INCLUDE PUBLIC SERVICE

You are probably wondering why so many of my stories focus on men. It is because men hold most of the power positions in the firms where I have consulted on leadership issues. As of this writing, here are some numbers that prove it:

- Only 4.0 percent, or 20 total, of *Fortune* 500 CEO positions are held by women.[1]

- Only 4.5 percent, or 45 total, of *Fortune* 1000 CEO positions are held by women.[2]

- *Forbes* reports only twenty women are running America's largest companies—and this is a record high.[3]

- Among publicly traded companies, just ninety-eight have women CEOs.[4]

Although we have a long way to go, we do see an increase in the number of women in workplace leadership. IBM, for instance, has broken its 100-year record and hired a woman CEO. And five newcomers to the top women leaders' list oversee more than $36.6 billion in revenues.

Women-owned businesses are also on the rise. According to the "2013 State of Women-Owned Businesses Report" commissioned by American Express OPEN, the number of women-owned businesses increased 59 percent between 1997 and 2013.[5] Their growth rate is 1.5 times the national average for all firms. Women have a strong presence in the health care and social assistance sector, where they represent 53 percent of owners nationally.

The report also notes that in 2011 the median proportion of female executives at successful companies was 7.1 percent, compared to 3.1 percent at unsuccessful companies.

A U.S. Government Accountability Office report indicates that 40 percent of workplace managers are women, although they earn just 81 percent of what their male counterparts earn.[6]

Not long ago, one large company found that 50 percent of its women employees were leaving the organization each year, a tremendously costly statistic. Consequently, to help increase its retention rate of these employees, the company brought in Menttium Corporation, an organization that provides mentorship services to women in the workplace. Founded in 1991, the company offers among its programs Menttium 100, which pairs mentors and mentees from different companies in six cities. After Menttium completed a mentorship with a senior person in the organization, the women stayed in their companies. The women now felt support, which was essential for their leadership. What interested me particularly was that the mentors were both men and women. Such mentorship programs have been gaining ground in America over the past few decades.

The Impact of Women's Cultural and Family Histories

Women's family messages have often been different from those of men because of their gender socialization. Women are typically socialized to be caretakers; many people would claim that women are socialized to be codependent. By *codependent,* I mean that many women have learned to defer to the needs of others to the neglect of themselves. At the same time, culturally, women have had permission to express their feelings, to be sensitive, and to be caring. Although these traits are often seen in family roles, they don't necessarily fall neatly along a clear line delineating men and women. I have never subscribed to the "men are" and "women are" theories of gender. In my experience, I would estimate that about 60 percent of women fall into the expressive, sensitive (high EQ) camp, while about 40 percent would fall into the task-oriented, low-expressiveness (low EQ) camp. The reverse could be said for men—I would estimate about 60 percent are task-oriented, with low expressiveness, and 40 percent are highly expressive, sensitive, and caring.

One interesting example is Sheryl Sandberg, Facebook chief operating officer (COO) and author of *Lean In,*[7] a book about women and leadership, who has said her siblings would tell you that as a child she was bossy and loved giving orders. At the same time, her parents insisted that, when she and her siblings had conflicts, they had to sit down and negotiate with one another. In her early family life, Sheryl learned behaviors that would serve her well in corporate America.

Recently I asked my daughter-in-law, Lorrie Warner, a health care executive, what early family messages shaped her leadership. She said that being firstborn might have something to do with the message that she was expected to be successful. She said in her early school years if she came home with a score of 92 on a test or paper, her father would ask why she did not get a 98.

Expectations for Lorrie were set in place before she was born. Her mother wanted her to be named *Lorrie,* but her father wanted the name *Lorraine,* because it would be better suited for a professional woman. She said she always felt the expectation that she was to be successful, but without any constraints. Lorrie also observed her mother's attention to detail, focus, and sense of direction. She said she "heard" messages from her dad but "saw" messages from her mother. Lorrie said that failure was never an option.

When I ask many women about their leadership styles, I hear that most have experienced both hierarchical leadership and team-based leadership and have found that the difference lies more in the personality than in the gender of the leader. The message I'm hearing is that there is much more evolution today around partnership and collaboration within and without companies where multidimensional leadership characteristics that result in success are in high demand today.

In contrast to Lorrie, Lois entered my executive women's seminar and admitted to a gnawing lifelong sense of shame and guilt that she was always "not quite enough." She was an established, highly successful physician in a large metropolitan city. She told her story from her first family in which the messages were clear. She told of the day her mother said to her, "I was happy the day you became a physician, but I was happier the day you married one." Lois's heart had sunk. Through the years, she had tried to show her parents that she was as good as her older brother, but he had been the "golden child." "I was never good enough," said Lois. With some help from the other women in the seminar, Lois realized that her mother's strong messages were the result of her *own* gender socialization: It was the man in the family who would provide. Her prefeminist messages to her daughter were that women came second. When Lois realized the historical context of her mother's messages, she was able to tell herself that those messages were about her mother and not about Lois or her fine success. She was able to transform her guilt, hurt, and disappointment into a mature understanding of the source of her mother's message.

Women leaders who have had abuse—sexual, physical, and emotional—in their family histories often take many years in identifying how it has affected them. Their trauma is buried beneath facades of competency and controlled through years of denial. Many times when I lecture on shame, women come up to me revealing that one of my stories tapped into their family abuse story from long ago. The number of women who have experienced some form of childhood abuse is startling. When I consulted at treatment programs for alcoholic women, I found that approximately 75 percent had been sexually or physically abused as children. Their no-talk rule from childhood follows them into their careers, where their "unfinished business" is often seen in the form of addictions, reactivity, false pride, mistrust, jealousy, resentment, narcissism, and codependency.

And yet, as leadership positions open up for women, we are mostly seeing success stories, as women transcend the cultural stereotypes and family role restrictions. As new generations benefit from the feminist movement's gains, more women come into the business and professional world free of the social and psychological baggage these stereotypes placed on them and able to develop their own leadership styles. Their leadership skills, in part, reflect the resiliency, skills, and positive personality traits nurtured in a flexible and supportive family system.

Leadership Styles of Women

Some researchers contend that few or no differences exist between the leadership styles of men and women; however, several prominent researchers have found strong gender differences. For example, the consulting firm Caliper Corporation assessed twenty-five thousand companies and found that the women leaders there were more assertive, more persuasive, and more willing to take risks than their male counterparts.[8] Other studies show that women leaders are more inclusive, open, consensus building, and collaborative. Studies in 2005 that looked at gender-role stereotypes found cultural myths are alive and well: women leaders were viewed as "less competent and yet emotionally warmer."[9] In contrast, the researchers found that the prevailing male gender stereotypes described male leaders as highly competent, tough, but lacking in warmth. The results of one 2005 study by the research firm Catalyst Inc. were summed up in its report title, "Women 'Take Care,' Men 'Take Charge': Stereotyping of U.S. Business Leaders Exposed."[10]

Facebook COO Sheryl Sandberg said in a recent talk that one reason women are not as successful as men is their attitudes about themselves. She cited studies that showed women not only underestimate their own abilities but also attribute their success to others—saying

"Someone helped me" or "I was lucky"—whereas men claim their success as the result of their own ability.[11] In leadership seminars I have conducted, I noted that women, more than men, are more often unaware of their strengths. A woman may have positive traits obviously seen by others, but because they are her particular innate traits, she herself is unaware of them. Many women leaders are much more aware of strengths they forge through personal-development work.

These findings may explain why women were perceived as working in a more participatory style, often seeking the wisdom of their peers and direct reports. That participatory style of work often translates into a transformative leadership style, with women being more supportive of their male staff than male leaders are.

Not all women are praised for their differences in style, however. A colleague who is the president of a small women's college recently told me that when conducting her board meetings with a group of high-powered, mostly male, executives, she senses she is only heard clearly when she communicates in the age-old "male" style, that is, in a tight, businesslike style with little time for any personal commentary. She said she had tried to be her authentic self, but did not feel she was being heard, so she adopted the style that works most efficiently for the board.

What is clearly evident regarding women's leadership today is that gender biases still exist. The glass ceiling, as it was so named in the 1980s, goes far beyond the ceiling. It is in the very structure of most corporations. And yet we're seeing more success stories among women leaders whose leadership styles are starting to change corporate culture. I recall consulting at the Corporation for the Northern Rockies, a foundation that supports the wildlife areas surrounding Yellowstone National Park. The evening speaker at our board retreat was the first woman superintendent of Yellowstone, Suzanne Lewis. She told the story of her first meeting with the longtime staff members, folks who knew much more about the park than she did. She asked each of them to tell about their role and how all was moving forward. There was only one woman in the circle besides herself.

Suzanne was a keen listener. After the meeting, the lone female staff person asked the men what they thought of the meeting. The group's consensus was that their new boss couldn't be very effective as a leader, because "she didn't tell us what to do!" Obviously the men were so accustomed to being led in a directive style that they did not know what to think of someone who trusted what they knew. Suzanne was employing a participatory leadership style. I recently followed up with her and she told me, "For the next nine years, I relied on the notion of being the first to give and the last to take when trying to lead during difficult and challenging times. I learned that you could never underestimate the power of generosity."

Deborah Szekely

Another woman who personifies the power of generosity is Deborah Szekely, founder of Rancho La Puerta in Tecate, Mexico, and the Golden Door in Escondido, California, two of the most acclaimed fitness spas in the world. Deborah, like leaders of many successful companies, has achieved remarkable success in moving each of her organizations toward being a "living company" by anchoring them in community. She is a case study for all the leadership qualities that women bring to organizations to challenge the stereotypical male-dominated, hierarchical models that have prevailed for decades.

Deborah's life and career have focused in three public arenas:

- in the modern health and fitness movement as cofounder of destination health spas

- in government, where she served as president and CEO of the Inter-American Foundation in Washington, D.C., and wrote the first management manual for members of both houses of Congress, *Setting Course,* now in its thirteenth edition

- as a philanthropist and public servant

Deborah has served her nation and community through her work in education, health and welfare, and the arts. She has created several nonprofit organizations, both locally and nationally, that flourished for many years, including The Combined Arts and Education Council of San Diego County and the Eureka Foundation. When asked how she has accomplished all these things, she said, "I just recognize a need, sell the dream, and help everyone else join in and make it happen."

Deborah's philanthropy and community commitment span many decades. As a young woman, she had a passion for the arts that took her to volunteering at the Old Globe Theatre in Balboa Park, San Diego, where she spearheaded the fund-raising of the Tony Award-winning theater for many decades. Deborah commented, "Volunteerism was my alma mater."[12] Always aware of community needs, she established the first school for the deaf in Tecate, organized a hot breakfast program in the schools, and founded Tecate's public library. She has continued working on cross-border issues. Her emphasis has been about helping people cope with poverty, making sure they have access to education and medical and legal services.

In her sixties, she moved to Washington, D.C. As president and CEO of the Inter-American Foundation for seven years, she developed new strategies to empower communities in Latin America and the Caribbean. Her leadership path continued in the 1980s when she was president of the International Volunteer Association. In 1998, she was named Outstanding Philanthropist by the San Diego chapter of the National Society of Fundraising Executives.

Deborah celebrated her firm's seventieth birthday. She is known for saying she has had more success than warranted. Her philosophy includes a strong belief in instinct and a belief that she is doing "God's work" in making people healthy.

Thanks to the Szekelys' daughter, Sarah Livia Brightwood (now president), Rancho La Puerta's efforts in sustaining the ecology and culture of the Tecate community have flourished. The resort's non-profit foundation—Fundación La Puerta—supports environmental, social, and educational projects, often with an emphasis on enhancing wildlife and native plants along the Tecate River. A 2,000-acre nature reserve was set aside as part of Rancho La Puerta's total 3,000 acres; it will be kept in a wild state in perpetuity and is a vital link in cross-border wildlife corridors.

The crowning glory of Fundación La Puerta is an educational center ("Las Piedras") used by local teachers as a classroom focused on natural history education and environmental awareness. The buildings are shaped like a cluster of natural boulders rising from a sea of fragrant chaparral. Surrounding Las Piedras is the town's largest park—Professor's Park—a donation by the Szekely family and the foundation.

The park is also an athletic, sports, and fitness mecca in the city of Tecate and hosts many cultural events, such as World Environment Day and Day of the Dead, each drawing many thousands of participants. Fundación La Puerta began drawing attention to the Tecate River ten years ago and initiated river cleanups that have contributed to the community's fabric, which now includes recycling initiatives, walking paths along the riverbank, and community gardens in marginalized communities along the river.

At ninety years old as of 2012, Deborah continues to champion new initiatives, and she maintains an extensive travel and public speaking schedule. She continues to work on the "side of the angels," as she describes it, and to share the learning from her many decades of community service.

This remarkable, energetic woman is an example of how a woman naturally concerns herself with creating and nurturing a sense of community. She has demonstrated genuine leadership by creating "living companies" where the employees feel like family. The fitness staff members live on the property; turnover is low. Employee scholarships are available for furthering education. Deborah lives with her late husband's favorite saying: "Siempre Mejor" ("Always Better"). An authentic leader to the core, she is a role model for all of us seeking to become genuine leaders.

Changing Cultural Stereotypes

One day I received a call from a leader in a major business publishing firm, who pitched me the idea of writing a book on the subject of women who outearn their husbands. It did not take me long to figure out that she was one of those women who felt guilt (and for some, it's shame) because she outearned her husband. I have never in my career heard any male consider outearning his wife to be an issue. The overriding issue here is gender socialization—and recent information suggests some of the long-ingrained stereotypes continue to (slowly) change:

- Many people now acknowledge that being a family's primary breadwinner has always been stressful, regardless of gender.

- The percent of women outearning their husbands (in families in which both the husband and wife have earnings) was approximately 29 percent in 2010.[13]

- One study shows that when women outearn their husbands, more of the men use erectile dysfunction drugs, and the wives often use anxiety meds. Although correlations are not considered causes by researchers, these correlations were not present in unmarried couples.[14]

- Men seem more willing to be in equitable marriages; many single women already outearn their male partners and have more parity.[15]

- According to a September 2010 article in *Time*, in all but three of the 150 largest U.S. cities, young women are making more money than men.[16]

These factors are challenging our gender-socialization messages. For example, a 2010 Pew Social Research Center survey showed 67 percent of Americans agree that to be ready for marriage, a man should be able to support his family financially, but only 33 percent say the same for women.[17] A 2007 Pew survey found that working mothers increasingly indicated they would prefer not to work full time.[18] Another piece of data that influences these figures is that 41 percent of children are born to single mothers.[19] While attitudes may reflect long-held values, these statistics suggest that the traditional family structure as we know it is at a crossroads today.

Regarding these changing percentages, I believe it's important to consider that when both people in a committed relationship or marriage can grow together, they have the opportunity of becoming and of fostering a fresh generation of genuine leaders. In light of these changes, it will be imperative that professional-development and personal-growth programs introduced into corporations include spouses and life partners.

Although many women throughout the world are still held hostage by being marginalized and disempowered, many leaders recently have stated that this century might well be called the women's century. The twentieth century saw female roles changing more rapidly than during any other period of history. In 1900, women were domestic creatures—wives, mothers, workers, and ornaments. Some had long sought new rights and freedoms. After a turbulent century with two World Wars and dramatic changes in technology, women had gained a vote and a voice.

Alice Eagly, a professor at Northwestern University's Kellogg School of Management, is a leader in women's leadership issues. She said that, according to her research, women usually fit into three distinct categories in their leadership—transformational, transactional, and laissez-faire. For models of these three categories, she uses Oprah Winfrey as transformational (optimistic, idealized influence, and inspiring), Michelle Obama as transactional (attends to problems when they become severe, such as obesity and health of children, and provides recognition for high performance), and *Vogue*'s editor Anna Wintour as laissez-faire (lack of involvement during critical junctures).[20]

In conducting leadership seminars, I have found that women are more likely to depend on their *real* power, their *personal* power, rather than their *role* power in their leadership styles. Perhaps because of gender socialization, women leaders draw upon a sense of high self-esteem, self-trust, and confidence, as opposed to using their title for their effectiveness. Yet genuine leaders—whether men or women—all shared one personal dimension: *personal power.*

Personal Power

Personal power is key to genuine leadership development. The root of the word *power* is from the Latin word *potere,* which means "to be able." Thus, the root of the word refers to the ability or capacity to perform or act effectively, a special capacity, faculty, or aptitude. We all have been born into power relationships—with parents, teachers, clergy, later with bosses and board chairs. But it is important to recognize that role power, based on people's titles and positions, is not *real* power. Role power allows strong influence, domination, and control. Personal power includes power as linking, in other words, competition with cooperation. Personal power also combines individualism with caring for others. To find our personal power, we act on what we know, we find our own feelings, and we choose to express them (or not). By now you can see the correlation with emotional intelligence. With personal power, as with emotional intelligence, we are connected with ourselves and thus can connect with others. David Whyte, a business consultant and poet, expresses it well in his poem, "The Journey" (from his 1997 book *The House of Belonging*).[21]

> Above the mountains
> the geese turn into
> the light again
>
> painting their
> black silhouettes
> on an open sky.
>
> Sometimes everything
> has to be
> enscribed across
> the heavens
>
> so you can find
> the one line
> already written
> inside you.

Sometimes it takes
a great sky
to find that

small, bright
and indescribable
wedge of freedom
in your own heart.

Sometimes with
the bones of the black
sticks left when the fire
has gone out

someone has written
something new
in the ashes
of your life.

You are not leaving
you are arriving.

Women Transforming Cultures

Women who do find their personal power often find their way in the business world when they are able to serve on corporate boards. Although many women in the United States do serve on boards, their involvement is typically on nonprofit boards or community organization boards. These service and community organizations cannot pay their board members. One way women have been supporting other women to reduce the board imbalances is through Women Corporate Directors (WCD), an organization for women holding *paid* corporate board positions. WCD is a group committed to supporting its more than two thousand members who sit on more than three thousand corporate boards. They work to advance participation of women on corporate boards, push for diversity on those boards, and advocate for and mentor women who are board members.

When I called Alison Winter, who cofounded WCD in 2001, I was curious to hear about her involvement with the organization. By the end of the interview, I realized she had much more to offer in her career story.

Alison, a chartered financial analyst (the gold standard in the investment industry), is truly a genuine leader who patiently made her way up the ladder at Northern Trust Corporation, a provider of banking, trust, and investment services. She became the company's founding president for Northeast Personal Financial Services from 2003 to 2006, copresident for Northeast Personal Financial Services from 2002 to 2003, and a member of the management committee from 2002 to 2006. In 2003, she founded and became CEO of Braintree Holdings, LLC, a private investments and consulting services firm.

In talking about her early years, she said she had no female role models. In her first full-time position at a large bank in San Francisco, Alison had completed all her coursework, yet the bank's attitude was that they could "not have a girl out there managing employees." Few companies back in the early 1970s were enlightened regarding women, and even fewer regarding minorities.

When she joined Northern Trust in Chicago in 1971, she considered herself fortunate to have the opportunity to work in a "great organization with a wonderful culture." The company was gradually changing in the early 1970s, even though it did not have any role models for her, nor any women in management. She recalls, "I was a good worker, had enormous capacity, and worked fast. I would say what I wanted, and they always offered me the female track." She persisted. As Alison tells it, "I kept holding out longer than many of the guys, and finally one of the heads of the investment units said, 'If she wants it that badly, she can come with me.'" Alison said that it probably took her an additional nine months to get moved. She also knew success would not be about how much she made in the short run, but how much she was learning, developing, that counted. "Then the rest will come," she said. Within a year, she was named an investment officer.

Alison went on to tell a remarkable story. When she was serving on the management committee, she recalls a time of major promotions across the organization. Yet not a single woman was promoted. She heard a great deal about this from women within the company and subsequently went to the CEO to let him know they had a big problem. She asked him if she could put a small group together to look at the actual facts of the progress of women during the past years, and he agreed. During the 1980s and 1990s, a major positive shift occurred in the percentage of women in successively higher levels of responsibility at Northern Trust. That trend stopped in the following decade, when there was little or no progress for women. When Alison and her group drilled down to look at the percentage of promotions from each pool of men and women, they found that the higher up the rank, the lower the percentage of women promoted. Another factor that was not immediately apparent was that at the most senior levels where a number of outside hires occurred, none were women.

To the managers' credit, an issue they had been unaware of before Alison's group investigated resulted in a new conscious effort to hire and promote the best people, with a strong, diverse mix. The CEO focused on the diversity of candidates in each promotion and held senior managers accountable to develop a diverse talent pool, so that the company would have great talent from which to promote. At times, if no woman or minority was on the promotion list for a major business unit, no promotions for that unit were made. The next quarter, the manager made sure there would be a more diverse group on that list!

Alison acknowledges that the initial lack of diversity was not a result of conscious discrimination; rather it was unconscious, as people tend to hire and promote people like themselves. Today, Northern Trust is very proud of the diversity of its people around the globe and the opportunity that diversity affords both the employees and the company.

Northern Trust is known as being focused on its community,

culture, and employees. In 2000, Catalyst Inc. gave Northern Trust its annual award "for the exemplary initiatives to advance women through their corporate ranks." Since 1990, the number of women officers increased from 39 to 49 percent; women of color represent nearly 36 percent of women officers and almost 17 percent of the total officer population. In addition, the number of women senior vice presidents rose from 6 to 28 percent, and the number of women at the executive vice president level and higher went from 0 to 24 percent. Northern Trust surely demonstrated what genuine leadership can achieve.

I asked Alison about Sheryl Sandberg's statement that what holds women back as leaders is their lack of confidence in themselves. Alison said that although it might have been true ten to twenty years ago, she thinks today there is less of that. She stated that women starting out might not feel highly confident, but as they meet certain milestones in their career, women in executive management surely have developed confidence. She added that many women do have to get past having an imposter syndrome, in which highly accomplished people continue to feel as though they are phonies or undeserving.

Now Alison is in her sixties, but when she left school, there were no expectations for women other than marriage and families. She said those young women who did go on to have careers surprised themselves. "Did we like more promotions, more opportunities, more money?" she said. "Of course!"

A noticeable change came with the women who entered the workforce in the 1980s and 1990s, women who had gone to business schools and who had grown up with Title 9, a 1972 educational amendment that prohibits gender discrimination in federally funded programs. Title 9 gave girls the opportunity to play competitive sports. Why did this matter? According to Alison, "Many companies looked for their leaders among people (meaning men) who played sports in school, as that was representative of people with a competitive drive to succeed; they understood what it meant to work as a team, and that the team was more important than one person. These women coming into the workforce had played sports, they were competitive, and they knew they wanted a career. They put these expectations on themselves, and in the process, they educated the managers that this was not their mother's workforce."

Although Alison said she had no role models, I asked whether she ever felt supported by women on her way up. She said several women were rising up the ranks with her, and they were a great support to each other. She also had several male mentors who were instrumental in her success. She said that although she hears some women say that other women blocked their progress, she never had that experience. And the senior women she knows in business across the country today have strong feelings about helping the next generation of women succeed to even higher levels.

Alison herself has been involved through the years in supporting the advancement of other women. By 1999, the United Way in the Chicago area was in the early stages of establishing the Women's Leadership Initiative to get more women to think of themselves as budding philanthropists by giving at leadership levels.

"We broadened it at Northern Trust, as a way for senior women to get to know up-and-coming women, so that we could promote them to others when opportunity presented itself," Alison explains. "I had an apartment that worked well for this. . . . We had an event every two to three months where we would showcase a group of women in a certain area and have them talk about what's going on in their field, such as investments, and what they recommended doing today." The women also adopted a women's homeless shelter. Among other activities, they collected soaps and shampoos from their travels and donated thousands of these items for women's shelters and women on the streets.

Alison was also a member (and subsequently chair) of The Committee of 200, a foundation supporting women in business leadership whose members are CEOs of major public and privately owned businesses. Often these women are the chief breadwinners for their families. So I asked Alison about women outearning their husbands.

She said whether it's an issue "depends on the parties in the marriage. Some couples succeed wonderfully by looking at this as a partnership, where they each use their highest and best talents and go for what they love to do and what is best for the overall family. Others find they are in competition with each other, and often two highly demanding careers can mean constant conflicts, and many end in divorce." In her own case, Alison's husband was bored with his own profession and took the opportunity to stay at home with their daughter and son for four years. He retooled his career to allow him to be available for the children. He found work that was fulfilling but not overly demanding on his time.

When Alison retired from Northern Trust in 2006, she did not really retire. She joined her business partner and colleague, Susan Stautberg, in ramping up the growth of Women Corporate Directors, the organization they cofounded in 2001. In 2006, they had five chapters; today they have fifty-two chapters around the globe. "That became a full-time job. [Eventually,] I decided that, with the birth of my grandchild, I wanted more time with family and friends. I am still engaged as chair emerita of the advisory board, treasurer, etc. So that was my second retirement." Alison is also still closely affiliated with Northern Trust as a mentor and serves on the board of the retailer Nordstrom as well.

Through the years, Alison has demonstrated the qualities of a genuine leader. She has exercised her personal power by speaking up to make changes and to lead in a participatory style to create new structures within organizations. She has a positive attitude, a keen self-awareness of her roots, and an equally strong understanding of how to support others in the process of change. Her investment in supporting other women shines throughout her career.

Women on Corporate Boards

Although some evidence suggests the glass ceiling is being shattered throughout the world, it is not happening in boardrooms. When we examine the data regarding women leaders serving on corporate boards, the figures are discouraging. The 2012 Catalyst Census revealed that in the United States the percentage of corporate board members who are women is 16.6 percent, up from 16.1 percent in 2011, a negligible difference.[22] Facebook COO Sheryl Sandberg said this low level of board participation by women occurs because of the lack of commitment on the part of the women leaders. She said women need to reverse their self-talk, explaining, "We [women] lower our own expectations of what we can achieve."[23]

Another obvious challenge is the "old boys' club" that continues to exist on many boards. Investment research analyst company Spencer Stuart announced that in 2012 there were 291 open director positions for S&P 500 companies (Standard & Poor's index of 500 leading companies), but hardly any were actually *open* because of the low turnover on public company boards.[24] Today women are serving on governance committees within companies to change the policies of board terms. One area in which we have seen major changes is in gender quotas being set for corporate board membership. Norway started with the requirement that all publicly held companies must have at least 40 percent women on their boards, not to exceed 60 percent. Other countries—including Spain, Italy, Belgium, the Netherlands, and France—have followed suit.

Something that has been overlooked in the addition of women to corporate boards is the influence of the male leadership. The former CEO of Campbell Soup Company, Douglas Conant, began mentoring women board members through an organization called The CEO Institute. Conant had been told by colleagues that they "just could not find women to promote at that level," to which he replied in a presentation at the 2011 WCD Global Institute, "There are women out there." Denise Morrison, the current president and CEO of Campbell Soup Company, was in The CEO Institute for fifteen years. Conant recommended Morrison for another company's corporate board. Conant recognized that the women they were grooming to be at the top at Campbell Soup could also contribute at other organizations and "would be top for their board." For senior executive women, this encouraging perspective about women serving on boards is a wonderful development. Although board service may not be an opportunity women can get within their own company, serving on boards of other corporations makes those individuals more valuable to their own company. Denise Morrison has also served as a board member for Ballard Power Systems since 2002 and Goodyear Tire & Rubber Company since 2005. Morrison is the twelfth leader in the 143-year-old Campbell Soup Company, and its first woman. She also belongs to several health-related food industry groups and is on the board of directors of Enactus.

As part of her transition to president and CEO of Campbell, Morrison was elevated to executive vice president and COO in October 2010 and earned a seat on the board. At the same time, she named a management team, which included the elevation of four key managers.

One of the things she is most proud of is her work with *Fortune/* U.S. State Department Global Women's Mentoring Partnership. Morrison has been named to *Fortune* magazine's "Most Powerful Women in Business" list. As part of that honor, she has been a member of a group of thirty-five women leaders "who give back to future business leaders." Denise Morrison is one more name in the long list of women changing the world of work for women.

Again, we see the story of a woman whose messages from her family were strong and early. From her father, she learned in grade school to set profit-margin goals, and from her mother, she learned that ambition is part of femininity. She left home with good skills for "leaning forward," in the words of Sheryl Sandberg, to become a genuine leader.

Women and Ethics

Peter Henning wrote in "Women Lead the Way in White-Collar Law," an April 2013 article in the *New York Times,* "But when it comes to researching and being an authoritative voice of study about white-collar crime, women are taking the lead."[25] Studies show that 94 percent of companies with three or more women on their boards had conflict of interest guidelines. It is interesting to note that only 58 percent of all-male boards have conflict of interest guidelines, according to an April 2009 article, "Women on Corporate Boards Makes Good Business Sense."[26]

When it comes to ethical decision making, several news-making and news-breaking stories have reported on women as whistle-blowers. Consumer advocate Erin Brockovich investigated the Pacific Gas and Electric Company in the 1990s after finding health issues and cancer were linked to chemicals in the company's wastewater. The firm settled for $333 million, followed by another payout some years later in the hundreds of millions of dollars.

Another whistle-blower was Sherron Watkins, vice president of corporate development at Enron, who was key in exposing Enron's accounting irregularities. Still another woman in the news was Cynthia Cooper, a vice president of internal audit at WorldCom, who uncovered a $3.8 billion fraud within that company. Watkins and Cooper, along with Coleen Rowley, an FBI attorney who uncovered pre-9/11 lapses, were named as 2002 Persons of the Year by *Time* magazine.

Another woman of courage was Lt. Gen. Claudia Kennedy, a three-star general, who exposed sexual harassment by a male general who was slated to oversee sexual harassment claims investigations in the armed forces.

Interestingly, some of these women had stay-at-home husbands, so their whistle-blowing held financial risk. Personal integrity, taking an ethical stand, is core to genuine leadership.

There are many other stories of women speaking up. Daniel Goleman reported on a whistle-blower study in which all those who spoke out did so because they had a deep commitment to the organization and to acting on their values.[27]

I recall a client calling me one day regarding her role in determining her future. As the sole executive woman on her prominent West Coast financial management firm's board and executive team, she had reviewed the tax portfolio of one of our country's national heroes. When she met with her four partners, she revealed that she could not sign the tax return because the numbers were not honestly reported. Her four partners told her clearly that she had no choice because of their client's prominence; they would risk losing their client. She was anxious, knowing that she had to take the right step in the right direction. There was no choice in her mind, but she knew she needed support for this difficult decision. She was very highly paid and knew she could be blackballed in the financial industry. After we spoke, she told her four partners that she had made her decision; she would not sign. She was ready to walk, knowing what a prized position she would be leaving—a position that had taken years of hard work to achieve. Obviously, the men knew she meant what she said. They valued her and her competence. Their final decision was to follow her lead, to hold the client accountable for honest reporting. This decision was a win-win for the firm, their leadership, and of course the client as well. The company could feel pride in their ethics; she kept a job she valued. And the client had a valuable education about ethics.

Another organization for women in leadership positions is the National Association for Female Executives (NAFE), an organization of twenty thousand members. In addition to offering programs for women leaders, the group ranks the top fifty companies for executive women's employment. These rankings are based on succession planning, profit-and-loss roles, gender pay parity, support programs, and work-life balance. For a company to qualify, it must have at least two women on its board and employ at least one thousand people. Many well-known organizations are listed on the NAFE website; Eli Lilly, for example, has been one of NAFE's Top 50 companies for the fifth straight year since 2009.

Challenges for Women in Leadership

Through the years, executive coach Lynn Banis of TurnKey Coaching Solutions has coached women in facing their challenges in the workplace. She states that although it is still a man's world, most women today (60 percent) do not feel that they need to act like men to succeed. I believe there has been movement away from the retrofitting concept, in which women are expected to take on stereotypically male traits to be taken seriously. Many studies show that women's leadership style results in more effective leadership, but Banis also cites some issues for women to address (with my comments in italics):

1. **Delegating.** Women still think they have to do it all by themselves. Skill in delegation actually makes a person a better leader and frees up valuable time to focus on the most important things.

2. **Negotiation.** Many women do not step up and negotiate for what they need in terms of resources. A leader cannot be shy or reticent about asking for and demanding what they need to get the job done.

3. **Balance.** This shows up in a couple of ways. Leaders need to balance their emotions with some peaceful interludes. Being in high gear all of the time takes a physical toll on people. The other aspect is work/life balance. This causes a great deal of stress and anxiety for a leader when they cannot make the decisions they need about their own balance issues.
   I recall one young executive woman telling me that anytime they had completed a successful "deal," she had to face what she had neglected at home—her husband and children. She was the only one on her team who did not have a stay-at-home wife.

4. **Emotions.** It is important for leaders to be passionate. Many women leaders are very passionate and they have to be sure that passion does not come across as anger.
   Gradually, there has been increasing permission to express emotions in the workplace. I still recall working with senior executives and teaching them four basic feelings: mad, sad, glad, and scared. Although most women are better at being expressive emotionally, I find that it is about a 60:40 ratio. About 60 percent of women are at ease with emotional expressions, and about 40 percent are not. Gender is not set in stone on this dimension!

5. **Guilt.** It is OK to ask for help. As a matter of fact, it is important to ask for help and to give it. Jobs are so big these days that no one can possibly do them all by themselves. Go to the smartest and best qualified person to get the help needed.

   Guilt seems to be an everyday companion for most women. Feminist theorist Rachel Hare-Mustin once said, "Show me a woman, and I'll show you guilt."[28] Most men do not feel guilty if they are missing a child's afternoon program at school or if they are late to keep a child's doctor's appointment.

6. **Voice.** Some women still have a difficult time finding their voice in the business environment. Part of that may be a self-confidence issue. The fact is that you were selected for the job you are in, and leaders are expected to speak up and be heard. Be prepared and add your value.

   When I led women's groups for leaders, the women practiced role-playing, strengthening their voices. In the earlier days, the women came to the group wearing trousers and even neckties, taking on the male model. When women could rehearse and practice, they definitely found their long-dormant voices.

7. **Self-Confidence.** Some leaders can be their own worst enemy. What you are doing is enough—it is probably more than what others are doing. You do influence people every day—step into it [self-confidence] and be intentional about how you influence. Believe you can and you will.

   People read one another on a constant basis, and they can easily read a lack of self-confidence. It is important to step into your self-confidence and trust that you can influence others. As one friend puts it, "If you don't vote for you, why would I?"

8. **Culture.** Women leaders, like all leaders, need to find a culture that supports their style, so they can be who they are and let their genius flow. Position yourself in a place where your clarity, confidence, and influence can make a difference.[29]

The Past Is Often Present!

Nadia came from an immigrant family in Chicago, and she had worked hard so she and her three siblings could have high-quality educations. Nadia's mother was not well-balanced emotionally and often would fly into irrational rages. Nadia, the second-eldest and the first girl, often stepped forward to protect her two siblings. She would speak up for them and get them out of their mother's way when she was in one of her fiery episodes.

When Nadia left home, she was relieved to leave all that behind her. She worked hard, in a near workaholic pattern. She received many awards and recognitions for her work in the finance field. When she reached her top executive position, as chief financial officer (CFO) of a multinational financial firm, she thought she had reached her pinnacle. Her family was proud of her. She had a good life, albeit with twelve-hour working days, but she had little time for relationships of any kind. Her work had become her primary relationship, a pattern not unlike those of her male peers. Yet she was the only one without a wife at home.

When her CEO brought in a new president to whom she would be reporting, Nadia's world began to fall apart. Her new boss would burst out in narcissistic rages when Nadia made errors on paper or in judgment. Nadia's style was to support her direct reports; they appreciated her. But now her work environment took a turn into a crisis-seeking system. Neither Nadia nor her reports could hold on to their confidence; they never knew when the president's next explosion might come. Nadia was highly stressed; she was trying to translate her reports' behaviors to the president, but he seemed to be impossible to satisfy.

Nadia finally decided to seek help. She knew she had to get leadership help or leave. She decided to attend an authentic leadership seminar for women. The weekend seminar was eye-opening and life-changing for Nadia. She realized that she had learned early in life to cope with her stressful feelings by working hard to bury her real feelings. She had received great rewards for her work patterns. But now she was forced to take a deep look into her family story. One of the sessions of the seminar was the re-enactment of a scene from her first family.

In the role-play, Nadia was reacting strongly to her mother, and the seminar leader asked her who else that might be in her present life. She immediately responded, "She's my boss!" Here, in the seminar, she could see how her current behavior at work was the same as it had been in her childhood, protecting the younger siblings, or in her office, her direct reports. Nadia had a great sense of freedom in "naming it." She realized she could walk away from her boss, could refuse to give him the power to hook her. She began to take her leave when he was disrespectful and rude in his outbursts. She also realized that her direct reports would need to deal with him themselves; she could no longer rescue every scene. In time, the president was relieved of his duties; the CEO called him "uncoachable."

Nadia went on to take care of herself and to support, but not "triangle" into, her direct reports' relationships. She was well on her way to genuine leadership.

Genuine leadership does not come easier for women than for men, but the issues they face might be quite different, often dependent on early life messages. But because of women's socialization in sensitivity and caring, women might indeed have an edge in starting the personal work necessary to become more genuine. Nadia's story illustrates that both men and women are able to "step into the light," as you will see in the next chapter.

Pathways for Change

The following exercise is a useful tool for further exploring the ideas from this chapter.

For Women Leaders: Mapping and Learning from Your Past

Here is the principal message of this book: our life stories reveal much about how we lead and where and how we learned to lead. When Bill George and Peter Sims wrote *True North: Discover Your Authentic Leadership*,[30] they learned that the 125 leaders they interviewed consistently stated that their purpose in leadership came from their life stories. By identifying people, events, and early life experiences that have had an impact on their ability to lead, genuine leaders can lead with a rich and deep understanding of who they are and what has shaped them. This can have special significance for women who have grown up in a culture that can still present roadblocks to a path to business leadership.

Using a large sheet of paper and crayons or colored markers, draw your lifeline. It need not be a straight line; our lives are never that! Allow your creative self to come forward and use images, icons (e.g., simple drawings, geometric shapes, or emoticons), and words to mark the significant people, places, and events from your childhood to your present age that have had some influence on how you see yourself as a woman and a leader. Every one of us has a unique story and no two are alike; there is no "right" path. Let the honesty in your lifeline show where you experienced what seemed to be failures or descents, and also let the line move upward when you met successes. Include here those who you think believed in your leadership abilities without seeing gender as a factor and those who didn't.

Create icons to characterize the major events that thrust you into your first leadership roles (e.g., a circle if it was a positive experience, a square if neutral, and a triangle if negative). Among the people you note, be sure to include your role models. With your lifeline before you, write a few paragraphs (or pages if you like) about what you learned from the people and the events that shaped your leadership as a woman. While we can identify our strengths here, it is also important to recognize what has shaped our "growing edges"—the areas in which we feel most challenged in our leadership. Now refer back to chapter 3, "Leading Change: Leadership Styles," and see if this exercise has given you more insight into identifying how you developed your leadership style and how your identity as a woman has influenced this journey.

Save your lifeline for reference when you fill out the Family Dynamics Questionnaire in chapter 7.

5

Finding Your Genuine Leader
[STEPPING INTO THE LIGHT]

"There are three things extremely hard:
steel, a diamond, and to know one's self."

— BEN FRANKLIN, SCIENTIST, INVENTOR, WRITER, AND
THE FIRST U.S. AMBASSADOR TO FRANCE

One of my mentors stressed the importance of finding yourself through your work, saying, "If you're not in it for your own growth, get out." What better edge is there than working with the power in your workplace, where you spend the greatest part of your waking hours?

First Steps: Finding Feelings

Many studies show that our intuitive strategies for regulating emotions ("Let's not talk about them") do exactly the opposite of what we intend, leaving us less capable of dealing with the world adaptively. Leaders who deal with intense emotions all day are often helped by developing techniques that truly keep them cool under stressful pressures.

Mark was the executive vice president of a *Fortune* 50 company when he invited me and my team in to train his senior leadership team in a "Creative Breakthroughs" training seminar series that focuses on self-awareness and communication skills. We immediately noted tension in the air, which surely granted little permission to express any feelings in the office. The culture reminded me of a cartoon showing an administrative assistant standing next to her boss's desk with a list of messages. She is saying to her boss, "Oh, and your feelings have been trying to get in touch with you." I smiled inwardly with this almost diagnosable warning; this obvious suppression of feeling was an easy clue to the participants' fear. I wondered what had caused them not to feel safe in their workplace.

During the consulting work, Mark received feedback from his direct reports' assessments about how "grim" he always appeared with his intimidating countenance. This feedback came at the same time Mark was turned down for an even higher position in his corporate ladder, leading him to a crisis of consciousness. He became motivated to know more about himself.

In telling his family childhood story, Mark recalled that he had been nicknamed "Happy" as a boy, because he always wore a grin or a smile. He related going off to New York City as a young man to advance his budding business career. Raised in a small, southwestern, rural town, he was also in search of business role models. What stood out to him when he arrived in the city was that no executives smiled; he inferred that businessmen are serious men. He immediately dropped his smile. He banished Happy from his life—at work and at home. "This is serious; this is business," Mark told himself. Mark's false self took on the persona of a committed, serious, "business only" executive.

None of his direct reports knew anything about his personal life other than that he had a wife and three children. He held all personal information closely. Mark joined his senior team members as we began skills training with the basic four feelings of mad, sad, glad, and scared. At first, I thought they would think we were too simplistic and feel insulted, but rather, they enjoyed learning a small feeling vocabulary and began to open their system's communication. Over time, they became more honest, more vulnerable, and more authentic with one another. The concept of integrity took hold in the system.

Mark became a fine role model as he learned to trust his direct reports. He began to reveal personal information about his life story and encouraged others to do the same. I recall a major step forward for Mark when we accompanied him to Europe to open a new plant—a plant in which they wanted to create a culture that welcomed expressions of emotions. When Mark introduced himself to the new workforce, he told his story of abandoning his smile and how phony he had always felt. He told how authentic he felt when he took "Hap" for "Happy" back into his life. His growth reminded me of an old Tibetan proverb that goes something like this: "When deep down inside the flame ignites, we light the way from inside." Mark was ignited. Mark had gone on to count the number of smiles in the executive suite. He learned that from childhood to adulthood, smiles decrease in frequency—by about 300 percent. He saw that in a safe environment, people smile at work.

As we worked together on many communication skills, Mark and his team could sense the changes they were making, and they became more trusting of the change process. Over time, these changes took hold and moved the entire division of the company forward into a model of true teamwork.

More about Emotional Intelligence

When Jared, a middle-management leader in a midsize, family-held engineering company, called for consultation, his voice revealed a lot. I could recognize within minutes that he had a very low EQ, because he informed me, "We don't do circles."

Researchers John D. Mayer, David R. Caruso, and Peter Salovey gave this definition of EQ in an article in the academic journal *Intelligence*:

> "Emotional intelligence refers to an ability to recognize the meanings of emotions and their relationships and to reason and problem-solve on the basis of them."[1]

They further expand the definition this way:

> "Emotional intelligence is involved in the capacity to perceive emotions, assimilate emotion-related feelings, understand the information of those emotions, and manage them."[2]

Jared was unaware of his feelings, could not recognize the emotions of others, and had little empathy for others. In our meeting with his senior-management team, the group decided it would be helpful for each of them to work on a personal development plan (PDP). Aware of the tools available, I used an EQ inventory with each member of the senior team.

In their team meetings where they shared their results with one another and committed to behavioral changes, they soon were able to communicate in new patterns. By recognizing and not judging their differences, they established new patterns of shared vulnerability and openness that revived their culture.

Jared, for the first time, showed his vulnerability to his direct reports; several times he choked back tears when telling his life story. What was obvious to the senior team, and eventually to the entire company, was that they now were led by an authentic leader. They were eager to go further and deeper. They talked about the integrity they felt by becoming more honest in their communication with one another. As a next step to explore, we talked about the concept of "mindsight," using reflection to integrate what we perceive and ultimately using our minds to change how we think.

Neuroscience and Mindsight

Neuroscience has entered the world of genuine leadership by showing us the involvement of the "quiet" signals in the brain. When the brain has a weak, or quiet, signal, the neural activity so necessary for better complex problem solving can occur. This research supports the stand of many leaders who take time to reflect when facing complex problems. Recent studies are stating that traditional brainstorming sessions, also called Type A brainstorming, in which more output and less input and reflection take place, are indeed quite ineffective; however, when pauses occur in brainstorming, many people find the sessions very useful.

Another finding from neuroscientists is that when a leader who is used to providing more output than receiving input gets feedback, the brain feels attacked. The person's brain perceives feedback as a threat to the person's status. This is one situation in which the concept of mindsight becomes useful in the world of leadership.

Mindsight is also the title of a book written by psychiatrist Daniel Siegel.[3] He has explored the role of the mind in mental health in his studies in interpersonal neurobiology. Through his research, he demonstrates it is never too late to integrate our impaired perceptions. As we focus our attention on the inner workings of our mind and make changes, the physical brain actually changes. It is possible to actually see these structural changes in the brain through brain-scanning technology.

Siegel states that about 20 percent of us walk around without knowing our own autobiography. In my consulting work with leaders, I would say the percentage is about 75 percent! As we expand our autobiography by exploring our family histories through tools such as genograms, we can open the door to deepening emotional intelligence. We can develop "mindsight," our capacity to use the mind to change the brain. Siegel advocates making sense of our lives by looking at our past as we deal with the present issues we face at work. By doing so, we can learn to "name and tame" our emotions rather than be overwhelmed by them.

From the Shadows and into the Light in One Generation!

Bill George and his son Jeff George are two leaders who have illuminated the path to genuine leadership for a generation. Their stories are in sharp contrast, however. Both are known as very successful leaders. Former CEO and chairperson of Medtronic, Bill is currently a professor at Harvard Business School and the author of the books *True North* and *Authentic Leadership*.[4] His son Jeff George is global head of Sandoz, a Novartis company. Jeff was named by *Fortune* on its list of top "40 Under 40" young business leaders in 2011 and 2012. Although the acorn fell close to the tree, the growth rings on that tree would read quite differently.

Bill's father gave Bill powerful messages in his early childhood, pointing his finger and saying, "You will be president of Coca-Cola!"

His father also identified IBM and Procter & Gamble as future possibilities. His father had been pushed aside as a leader, and he wanted to be sure his son was not.

Bill inherited his father's fear of being rolled over. Bill said that he clearly started out by trying to make up for his father's failures and to pursue his dreams as well. He felt caught between his father's messages of fulfilling those dreams and his mother's wish for him to be who he was. One gift of Bill's being an only child was his interactions with and his capacity to relate to high-level adults. He revealed that at age twenty-three he was comfortable when dealing with people at the U.S. Department of Defense, but his peer relationships were more difficult.

Bill began his leadership track in high school by running for leadership positions—and losing. In college he continued his pursuit; he ran many times for offices, including for the office of fraternity president. Again and again, he lost. Finally an upperclassman told him no one wanted to work with him. With this candid feedback, Bill worked on his leadership skills and eventually became fraternity president.

As Bill moved along in his career, he learned that he was working with a pattern of intentional intimidation; he said he had difficulty working well with people who were using power over him. His disadvantage was that he could get hooked—and he would argue back reactively. He often took stands for others when bullying leaders would pick on the most vulnerable person in the room. He saw how tyrant leaders would take on the weakest person in the room; he saw that they had the skill to draw people in and find their vulnerability. Bill also admitted to then using his own form of intimidation to challenge these leaders—the style he learned from his father.

Bill said he never felt like he belonged in the men's club. He did not drink scotch or play golf or poker. To hide his fear of being rejected, he tried to appear invulnerable and came off as very independent and strong. Although he always knew he was good enough to do his job, he never felt that he was a "member of the club," often feeling he had to hide his passions and his values.

When Bill became CEO of Medtronic, a medical and cardiac device company whose values he shared, he felt he could "walk his talk." Bill began his personal work quite early, but he had to learn to have empathy for many of the leaders he had joined along the way. He worked through his issues and began meditating and reflecting deeply on his own family crucibles. Today, in his course on leadership at Harvard Business School, the students explore their own crucibles in their histories. Although students are aware of the personal aspects of the course, the course is still among the most requested at the school.

In hearing Bill's story, I was deeply impressed to learn of all the personal work he did to become an authentic leader who went on to write *True North*. Bill surely had the courage to face his past, as well as delve into his present life and leadership style.

Today Bill George can be vulnerable; he has said vulnerability is power that both binds and bonds us, explaining, "If I can express my vulnerability, you no longer have power over me ... and if I try to hide from you, then I cannot be real and I give you the power."[5]

A Systemic Shift!

Bill's son, Jeff George, grew up in a very different environment. His parents encouraged personal growth and development—a sharp contrast to his father's upbringing. Jeff's rise to leadership at Sandoz in his thirties has been dramatic. He is in charge of twenty-five thousand employees across 140 countries, leading the second-largest generic-drug company globally. Jeff began his "crucible" search early in life. He said that his ability to be vulnerable makes it okay to bring his whole self to work. Jeff has cried in front of others, thus giving them permission to bring the "who I am" to work and creating a robust culture.

Although Jeff said he is comfortable revealing his emotions, he knows well enough when *not* to show his vulnerability (e.g., to some senior officers in the industry). He has received positive feedback about his leadership style. He said this validates him: "It brings me alive." Jeff talks about the years of therapy and coaching he had in self-realization and self-awareness. When meeting in retreat with his senior group, he uses literary and spiritual sources, such as the work of Kahlil Gibran, author of *The Prophet,* on sorrow and joy.[6]

While Jeff did have a family culture that was supportive, he still struggled. Born to a powerful CEO father and a psychologist mother, he faced his own issues. He recalled one professional telling him what he needed to hear, "Jeff, you are good enough," and that feedback helped him move forward. Jeff's path took him to making key decisions regarding his education, his self-development, and his career choices.

Today Jeff meditates daily, has several coaches, and states that both approaches have made a profound impact, allowing him to be warmer and more integrated, empathic, and vulnerable. Jeff is proud of changes he has been able to make at the headquarters of a traditionally German organization, which as of this writing has employees of more than forty-two nationalities (including eight among his direct reports). He is interested in spirituality and energy meditation. He trusts his intuition and uses it widely in his work. He believes that all those he works with have untapped gifts. He was appreciative when hired, because he was told, "You're a growth guy."

When I asked Jeff how he handled the loneliness of leadership, he explained that he has self-imposed boundaries but is able to be closer with his direct reports than the generation before him. Although Jeff consults his direct reports closely on most topics, he finds it important to have a small group of mentors and coaches outside of work (what I call a personal board of directors) to whom he can turn for alternative perspectives, particularly when he's feeling weighed down.

Regular workouts—he runs three to four times per week—are important to Jeff, as is regular massage and focusing on body, mind, and spirit to guide his leadership. Jeff believes that his mother made a great impact on his growth and said it is "great that Dad is open."

These contrasting, yet complementary, stories reflect the importance of "going home" and understanding how our first families shape our growth in becoming genuine.

For the Greater Good: Corporate Social Responsibility (CSR)

Genuine leadership and genuine leaders like Bill and Jeff George often take the valuable step of initiating corporate social responsibility (CSR) in their companies. This move is not surprising when we look at some of the characteristics people widely acknowledge in describing genuine leaders. From Imagemakers International, a Toronto-based leadership development company, come these characteristics of genuine leaders:

- Their values define who they are and how they live their lives.

- They are real, and others say they are real.

- They respect themselves and others, and they really care about those they lead and interact with.

- They project the essence of who they are from the inside out.

- They lead by example and have values that cause others to emulate them.[7]

Genuine leadership, then, is not about leading others; it is about how one leads oneself. It is a way of being and, most importantly, a way of life.

What is exciting today is to see the number of genuine leaders who have taken their values of authenticity, caring, and respect to lead their companies to the highest levels. Their values are reflected even in taking relatively modest paychecks compared to their peers. Jim Sinegal, the recently retired CEO of Costco, had a salary of just $350,000 (excluding bonus and stock options); this was shocking to many American CEOs. His replacement, W. Craig Jelinek, is earning $650,000 plus stock options and bonuses, which is still at the lower end in corporate salaries overall.

Sinegal's own paycheck was modest; he treated his employees well. It is not uncommon for a high school graduate working at Costco, over time, to earn in the $40,000 range. And more than 80 percent of Costco employees have competitively priced health plans. In addition, employees show high job satisfaction and tend to stay for many years. If someone bought Costco stock a decade ago, they would find its value has tripled in this last decade. It is easy to see how Costco is a leading corporate social responsibility (CSR) retailer in the United States (it ranked in the top fifty in 2011).[8]

The Corporate Social Responsibility Index (CSRI) rates companies on three key dimensions: citizenship, governance, and workplace.[9] This combined score gives the public insight into the influence of the company's programs and policies on their reputations.

The CSR movement began in the 1960s as a form of corporate self-regulation integrated into business models. The leaders wanted to integrate social, environmental, and governance practices that would be self-regulating business monitors, ensuring compliance with the spirit of the law, ethical standards, and international norms. CSR advocates declare that such corporations not only "do the right thing" but also can change how business is practiced—all for the greater good.

Many companies approach CSR through corporate philanthropy, setting up funds for nonprofit organizations and communities. They often give in areas such as the arts, education, housing, social welfare, health, and the environment. I have found in my consulting work that employees carry a sense of pride when they know that their company has a high CSRI score. Many of these companies—including The Walt Disney Company, Johnson & Johnson, Microsoft Corp., Google Inc., and General Mills—are consistently top performers. When genuine leaders who have embraced the value of self-awareness, including their family influences on their emotional life, can lead a company with a high CSRI, the path to making changes in our entire culture can open.

Pathways for Change

The following meditation and genuine leadership quiz provide useful tools for you to continue to explore the ideas from this chapter.

Meditation

Since leaders need to be fully aware and alert as well as productive, many turn to caffeine, long hours, and eating on the run. Others have learned that with meditation, they can reach a state of "restful alertness." Brain research validates that meditation actually improves brain functioning, and thus performance. Meditation also decreases blood pressure and heart disease and lowers cholesterol. Hundreds of companies now include mindfulness meditation in their offices. Jon Kabat-Zinn, founding director of the Stress Reduction Clinic and the Center for Mindfulness in Medicine, Health Care, and Society at the University of Massachusetts Medical School, reminds us that after eight weeks of meditation, structural changes in the brain can be seen.

Take time to incorporate meditation into your daily life, even in the workplace. Psychiatrist Daniel Siegel has several guided imagery exercises available online (http://drdansiegel.com/resources/everyday _mindsight_tools/). Health Journeys (www.healthjourneys.com) is also a source of guided imagery CDs and MP3s.

Genuine Leadership Quiz

1. Name the most authentic leader you have interacted with in the past seven years. (It need not be a renowned person or high-profile person.)
2. Why did you select him or her?
3. What additional attributes of the person are important?
4. How would you evaluate yourself on the attributes you have listed?

5. What must be done to improve your lowest scores?

6. What causes your "dark moments"—your "moments of gravest concern"?

7. What do you do at those times?

8. How would people who watch you lead describe your highest priority? (How do you explain any differences between their observations and your response to question 4?)

9. What experiences had the greatest impact on your authentic leadership behavior?

10. What do you want from principled followers?

11. What do you do to encourage authentic followers and authentic leaders?

12. How would (or how do) you develop authentic leaders and authentic followers?

After answering these twelve questions, find a quiet time and place in which to write what you have learned about your genuine leadership. Include the shadow side that you are working on, the aspects that you feel you have outgrown, and the challenges you still face. Then, write a letter to yourself. Describe where you are, what kind of leader you have become, what growth has occurred, and what challenges you faced. Put your letter in a safe place. If you have a personal board of directors, schedule a time six to twelve months from now to meet with them. At that meeting, read your letter aloud. This can be very revealing about your progress and your path ahead.

6

The Way Through

[COMPANY CULTURES IN FLUX]

"Culture does not change because we desire to change it.
Culture changes when the organization is transformed; the culture
reflects the realities of people working together every day."

— FRANCES HESSELBEIN, FOUNDING PRESIDENT AND
CEO OF THE FRANCES HESSELBEIN LEADERSHIP INSTITUTE,
AUTHOR OF *LEADER TO LEADER* AND OTHER BOOKS

By learning how some genuine leaders lead their organizations, we've already looked at the beginnings of a workable, practical model that shows the way to create a positive, adaptive, resilient culture. The process requires changing the behaviors of the leadership, not only at the top but also throughout the organization.

The model begins with personal change. As Peter Senge, director of MIT's Center for Organizational Learning, has said, "The more we change, the more we change the system."[1] On an individual level, this includes facing and exposing the shadows that have shaped the self, while exploring one's personal contributions to that workplace culture. Next, with the new awareness from facing the shadow side, the transitional process can begin. This stage consists of "finding your true north"—facing your own crucible as Bill George did, and along with that, acknowledging the influence of one's first family. Learning emotional intelligence skills, as we've seen, is also critical.

Of course, we cannot assume that if all leaders face their shadows and develop their emotional intelligence and authenticity, they will find the direct route to their core, their true integrity, their ethical behavior, and organizational success. But the opportunity *is there* to create a thriving, positive environment with clearly recognized cultural values. Genuine leaders can lead by releasing caring human energy in the workplace.

Preventing an Organization's Early Demise

The daily news reminds us of corporate cultures that illustrate just the opposite; they are driven by power, narcissism, and greed. And we've already seen some of the costs to organizations for maintaining such inhumane and unsatisfying cultures (as illustrated in Michael's story in chapter 1 and other stories in this book). Another cost may be the shortened life of corporations. Recent findings show that 95 percent of small companies will close their doors after five years; 50 percent will fail within the first year.[2] Even the average life expectancy of a multinational corporation—*Fortune* 500 or its equivalent—is between forty and fifty years.[3] Many in our population have so normalized this short-term perspective that they say, "Well, isn't that how capitalism works: 'Make your money and move on'?" To that question, most genuine leaders would respond, "Absolutely not!"

These early organization death rates affect not only individuals' employment but also their family lives and their communities, since finding new work often requires uprooting families. When companies can change their organizational cultures by addressing some of their core leadership issues, they can also change the early death rates of their organizations. Leaders who choose to face their shadow sides can develop resiliency more readily, more effectively. Throughout this book, I've shared success stories of those who overcame overwhelming odds and family crucibles that were setups for failure. These stories describe dramatic and courageous change—change with the possibility of transformation, which implies a renewed organization.

The Center for Creative Leadership, in its studies and experience, has found that transforming cultures is not an easy task, for these reasons:

- Bigger minds are needed to keep pace with rapidly changing reality.

- Change requires new mind-sets, not just new skills.

- Hidden assumptions and beliefs must be unearthed.

- Organizational change requires leaders to change.

- It takes a new kind of hard work. Stop calling them "soft" skills.[4]

I have often heard employees say, "Well, I have learned that the 'soft stuff' is really the 'hard stuff.'" These soft skills are hard, because they are the people skills that genuine leaders instill in their organizations to create what organizational learning expert Arie de Geus calls a "living company."[5]

Becoming a "Living Company"

"Companies die because their managers focus on the economic activity of producing goods and services, and they forget that their organizations' true nature is that of a community of simple humans."

— ARIE DE GEUS, FOUNDING MEMBER OF THE SOCIETY FOR ORGANIZATIONAL LEARNING

In *The Living Company: Habits for Survival in a Turbulent Business Environment*, Arie de Geus wrote about his discovery in response to these questions: "Why has business not taken its place as an American institution?" and "Why does business have such a high death rate?" He gave the name of "living companies" to those that "allow themselves to evolve," those that, like other institutions, value and implement new ideas and new people. He reminds us that assets are like oxygen—necessary *for* but not the *purpose of* life—and has said, "These companies will continue to renew themselves through the years, much like family systems do." The retired director of corporate planning at Royal Dutch Shell, de Geus responded to the startling issue of poor corporate longevity by saying that the answer is *people,* not financial assets.

In *The Living Company*,[6] de Geus describes four basic characteristics of a successful living company:

- a sensitivity to the surrounding environment—taking careful note of what is happening

- a strong identity in which a company builds a community

- a tolerance for building diverse relationships within and without the company as the company grows

- conservative philosophy in its financing, effectively governing for growth

Marjorie Kelly, coauthor of *The Divine Right of Capital: Dethroning the Corporate Aristocracy*,[7] supports the living company philosophy. She writes that when companies focus on making profits for stockholders to the exclusion of everyone else's interests, that is actually a form of discrimination based on property or wealth. For far too long, it has been taken for granted that stockholder earnings are the proper measure of a company's success. Fortunately, this perspective may be changing today. If unethical behaviors were paralleled by poor profits, perhaps more businesses would seek change much sooner. Unfortunately, no direct correlation has existed between financial success and a healthy, respectful workplace. Kelly has argued for a new model of the corporation as human community, with both external and internal constituents to whom it must be accountable.

Too often leaders have not known the line between wealth and greed. Profitability and shareholder value have been considered the indicators of corporate success and health.

Yet at the same time, longevity has *nothing* to do with a company's material assets, its industry, or its productivity! Our leading business schools and the financial community have joined in this fallacious thinking that wealth comes first. With this focus on economics and financial returns, most companies have neglected to focus on the very basic fact that many authors have been addressing: *A company is a community of humans.* Two American firms come to my mind when thinking of a community of humans. First is IBM, now more than one hundred years old. IBM hires for character, not just top résumés. And at Southwest Airlines, now in its forty-fifth year, getting hired there is as difficult as gaining entrance to Harvard, Yale, or Princeton.

The character and values of any organization are determined primarily by the few people at the top. The dynamics of a company are shaped by the assumptions and beliefs of the senior leaders in management, as well as the leaders in smaller arenas throughout the workplace. The neglect of focusing on the community of humans has resulted in companies losing literally billions of dollars in revenue, productivity, and efficiency.

If companies want to focus on their human community, they will need to focus on *who we are* at work. Mike Robbins, author of *Focus on the Good Stuff: The Power of Appreciation,* said that, according to statistics from the U.S. Department of Labor, 64 percent of people left their workplace because they did not feel appreciated.[8] This is just one example of where the renewal can begin.

When reading the statistics about the U.S. work environment, I find they support the cultural diagnosis I have given to many firms who don't fit the living company profile: spiritual flatness. Most of us have experienced walking into a workplace where there is negative energy. Such an energy drain squelches creativity, creates isolation and insecurity, and drives behaviors that cost the company financially. This "toxic energy" can be felt in the boardroom or the pulp mill, the checkout line or the airline ticket counter. Toxicity is very democratic regarding place, salary, status, or title. The issues are the same: whether we are the CEO, the bookkeeper, electrician, or support staff, we all face human issues at work. All too often I have seen people leave one workplace and enter another only to face similar, if not the same, issues.

Relationship Trust

All the research studies on what makes the difference between healthy and toxic workplaces agree that the most important factor between the leader and those being led is the issue of trust. Trust is based on integrity. U.S. business magnate Warren Buffett said it well: "Trust is like the air we breathe. When it's present, nobody really notices. But when it's absent, everybody notices."[9]

Any leader's first job is to inspire trust! Author and leadership authority Stephen Covey stated that trust is built on competence and character. He said competence includes a person's capabilities, skills, and track record, but character includes integrity, motive, and intent.[10]

Because so many corporate leaders are still out of touch with their personal histories and bring their family dysfunction to the workplace, it is easy to see how only 49 percent of employees trust their senior management, and only 38 percent believe their CEOs are a credible source of information.[11] The effects are widespread and costly. Our low-trust culture has cost us greatly. The Association of Certified Fraud Examiners estimates that the average company loses 5 percent of its annual revenue to some sort of fraudulent action.[12] We see these stories almost daily in the local and business media. The firm of Watson Wyatt has found that high-trust companies outperform low-trust companies by 300 percent.[13] That figure would motivate any senior-management person!

Stephen Covey found through his work with trusted leaders throughout the world that high-trust leaders demonstrate these thirteen behaviors:

1. Talk straight.
2. Demonstrate respect.
3. Create transparency.
4. Right wrongs.
5. Show loyalty.
6. Deliver results.
7. Get better.
8. Confront reality.
9. Clarify expectation.

10. Practice accountability.

11. Listen first.

12. Keep commitments.

13. Extend trust.[14]

Leaders who balance their self-trust with relationship trust can inspire others in becoming genuine leaders.

Unfortunately, a high percentage of fear-driven and dysfunctional, shame-bound leaders still are unwilling and resistant to make the essential, meaningful, sustainable change required to build trust in their organizations. It will be unlikely for these changes to take place in corporations until we see the transformations of the dysfunctional leadership. It *is* happening, however.

Creating the Reality: Ethics Rising

Of course, as many of the profiles in this book show, there are leaders who are mature, strong, ethical human beings leading companies in positive directions. In leading change, corporate leaders have improved the professional and personal lives of countless employees and their families. One memorable story comes from Zyg Nagorski, founder of the Center for International Leadership, who believed that ethics can be taught. Throughout his career, he worked with senior executives on their moral decision making, using writings by Aristotle, Plato, and Abraham Lincoln. The executives were challenged by this Polish émigré to work on their reflection and their decision making, facing their own barriers. When I worked in a three-day seminar with Zyg, he told an inspiring story that concerned a CEO and his sales manager who had just sold the manufacturing firm's largest contract. Zyg said the sales manager explained that there was one glitch; the Chinese workers on the equipment would range from seven to ten years of age, which presented human rights concerns. According to Zyg, the CEO returned the contract to his sales manager, saying, "It's up to you; *you decide!*" The sales manager did not hesitate; he tore up the contract.

This CEO, as Zyg reminded us, showed that he was walking the talk; he was able to promote integrity in his leadership team members by trusting that they knew what was the right thing to do. Obviously, financial gain was not primary; living the company's values on a global scale mattered. What stood out for me was how the management team members had learned to integrate their authentic selves into their roles. They also held a shared pride in this story of ethical cultural behavior.

It is sad, though, that the number of stories of corruption eclipses stories of genuine leadership in the media. Of course, we cannot escape reading and hearing about the Enrons, the Madoffs, Wall Street and the recession, the recent JPMorgan losses and regulatory issues, the McKinsey fraud charges, and financial fraud depicted in the award-winning documentary film *Inside Job*.

During the 1990s and into the 2000s, many firms established ethics officer positions. Currently, more than 150 corporations have ethics officers—surely a step in the right direction.

And for every Enron, there is a Mike Loftin or a Betsy and Jesse Fink. Let's look at these leaders who transformed their organizational cultures to became a living company through genuine leadership.

Homewise: A High-Functioning Company

At a time when housing issues, such as mortgage defaults after job layoffs, mishandled foreclosures, and tightened lending practices, have devastated millions of homeowners in America, Homewise in Santa Fe, New Mexico, is one organization that has held up steadily to keep families in their homes and to help others purchase new homes. Homewise has provided housing for moderate-income families since 1986. Led by Mike Loftin, a visionary executive director, Homewise has had remarkable growth since he joined the organization in 1992—from having less than $1 million to $61 million in assets, and going from three employees to forty.

With Mike on board, Homewise expanded its services to include home purchase, home repair, one-on-one financial counseling, homebuyer and financial literacy classes, real estate sales services, and development of affordable energy- and water-efficient homes. Homewise is also a community development financial institution, providing mortgage lending, home improvement, and refinance lending for its customers. With its focus on financial security through homeownership, Homewise has helped more than 2,300 people purchase homes and more than 1,675 people keep their homes by providing financial and technical assistance for home repair. In addition, Homewise has trained and counseled more than 8,200 people toward successful home ownership and has built more than 440 quality affordable homes. Homewise homes are built to the highest green standards for the state of New Mexico and the city of Santa Fe. All Homewise services, including the home buyer education and financial literacy classes, are available in English and Spanish to serve the entire community.

Inspired by talking with business leaders in the community, in particular the public school superintendent and the local hospital CEO, Mike's group created the Santa Fe Business Campaign for Homeownership. Homewise partners with businesses in the community, offering to come into the workplace and talk about Homewise services to their employees. This has resulted in Homewise's working with more than 170 Santa Fe businesses, providing the opportunity for quality, affordable homes to teachers, police officers, working single moms and dads, and many others in occupations at the middle-income pay level.

With its mission of financial security, Homewise can boast a delinquency rate lower than prime, Veterans Affairs (VA) and Federal Housing Administration (FHA) loans, and only one foreclosure during twenty-seven years of business. And Homewise walks the talk in its own home. Mike Loftin has created a business model, the HomeSmart model, that not only assists customers with financial security but also provides the company with an operational self-sufficiency ratio of 100 percent—remarkable in the world of nonprofits.

With this model, Homewise is expanding in New Mexico, and Mike is taking the model to other affordable housing organizations throughout the country. Inspired by his family story—seeing his mother struggle to buy and keep their family home—Mike is deter-mined to help moderate-income families in the United States know that the dream of homeownership is still alive—and is possible.

Mike's decision to enter the homeownership industry is probably no coincidence. He grew up in a family with alcoholism, secrets, and divorces. His father lost his job at PNM, the local electrical utility company, his parents divorced, and his father died at age forty-seven. Like many men in his age group, he smoked a lot, drank heavily, and had heart problems. Mike's mother held down two jobs to hold the family together. Mike recalled his mother's living in fear that the IRS would take their house. Later on, the house was saved and his mother paid it off. She still lives in the house where Mike grew up, and today she can live comfortably because she owns the house.

I asked Mike how he managed his power. He said through being the visionary, being committed, taking risks, and being an implementer. When I asked why anyone would follow him, he said, "Because I do try to do the right thing." Admitting to being impatient, Mike said his employees would also say he is a visionary, has high expectations, is judgmental, and is always trying to get better.

Betsy and Jesse Fink

Through the years, most leaders have seen that a leader's age is not a deterrent to a company's cultural transformation. Gradually I have witnessed a variety of unexpected behaviors in the workplace. Flexi-bility is not for the young alone. Genuine leaders of all ages have led the way in transforming cultures. Such is the story of Jesse and Betsy Fink.

When I interviewed Jesse Fink about his genuine leadership, I found that after he told me about his early life leadership experiences, the conversation went quite quickly from "me" to "we." Betsy and Jesse Fink have truly operated as a team throughout their marriage and work partnership—with complementary leadership styles. Jesse Fink has been the exterior face of their leadership; Betsy Fink has been the internal engine. Jesse and Betsy advise young people today to follow their passion. This is exactly what they have done.

Leadership seemed to come quite naturally to Jesse, and his history is one of gravitating toward leadership opportunities with the help of many role models and mentors. His first leadership roles were as head of the honor society in high school, followed later by resident assistant (RA) in college. Both roles involved leading a peer group, which has its special set of challenges. He gained trust and respect by showing he cared about the people.

One of Jesse's first leadership role models was a science teacher in high school, a passionate environmental teacher who took the students on expeditions. Through examining issues at the school, in the community, and around the world, this teacher was able to motivate students to get excited about environmental issues. For two summers in high school, Jesse volunteered with the Student Conservation Association, his first team experience. The work took him to national parks, where he worked on a trail crew with ten others; they learned to work together. Jesse said that during that first summer he observed outstanding leadership from a married couple who worked together in the outdoors. Jesse learned how a married couple partnered, each bringing complementary skill sets to successful joint leadership. This couple served as a role model for Jesse and his marriage.

After graduating from college in the 1970s, Jesse had a summer job as a supervisor of young adults who would have been categorized as "troubled youth," and he had to earn their respect to get them to work together. After college, at age twenty-one, he worked for Georgia-Pacific in South Carolina and supervised two staff people and many crews who worked as contractors. He said he remembered the crews "checking out" this twenty-one-year-old college kid from New York. Eventually he did earn their respect and their trust, despite the fact that often on Friday afternoons or Mondays he had to find them!

When Jesse went back to the Whitman School of Management at Syracuse University for his MBA degree, he was an assistant director of housing with eight to ten RAs reporting to him—again he was leading a peer group. They were all full-time students and part-time RAs, so learning to lead around time management and collaboration issues was key to his success.

Jesse then worked at Citibank for three years. He said he learned more there toward his professional development than he learned from anyone else through the years. One message he took that influenced him greatly was his boss's ability to care about people. After that, he worked in an assortment of marketing and management positions until Jay Walker recruited him to be COO of Walker Digital and then cofounding COO at Priceline. Jesse said those were constantly changing days. Since Priceline was one of the few Internet companies on the East Coast, Jesse joked that his job came down to people, space, and food. Changes were coming so rapidly with their constant growth that they were always looking for new space. Food was how they kept people there. Jesse was interested in people and wanted them to be satisfied and happy. He said there was no playbook to follow; every day presented a new crisis.

Jay Walker, the founder of Priceline, was the external face of the company, but from Jesse's earlier work experiences, he had become adept at leading from behind. With a strong management team of industry experts, Jesse's role was to be the heart and soul of the company. He said they always could "figure it out by hiring inexperienced, passionate people, often young kids, and by having them do extraordinary things." From 1995 to 1997, their employees felt safe and competent and secure—and the managers could push them. The leaders gave the employees permission to make mistakes.

Jesse asked Betsy to join him as Priceline's fourth key employee. She had worked for the online service Prodigy for several years and knew interactive media and was involved in creating Priceline's user-interface experience. Beyond that, she had a calming influence on these young people, helping them to move forward. Hers was a strong, grounded leadership. Betsy had a natural sense of using space, and to this day she creates spaces and builds experiences that continue to inspire and lead individuals and communities. Together Jesse and Betsy continue to focus well on people, space, and food!

After I had sent Jesse his story for this book, he sent back a remarkable email, which I include here:

Marilyn, having [some time] to think about the power and message of your book, I can pull the various aspects of my personal and professional experience together. I think leadership is about purpose, passion, and authenticity. I have had many leadership roles in my life, and when the goal of the organization was aligned, I was successful. There might be times when one of the above is slightly off the curve, but in the long run they need to be aligned.

I think a best example is my tenure as COO of Priceline when we went from Jay Walker's idea to a small start-up, to a fast-growing Internet company, and to an IPO. We had Monday morning meetings, and I ran them. I would stand up and do all I could to inspire and empower our amazing team. There were times when our organization was fragile, stressed, and running on fumes. But when I stood up and encouraged teamwork and passion, it seemed to be some of the fuel needed to get through the week. I was honest and transparent, and the passion and love I had for the organization was worn on my sleeve. We all did whatever we could to move toward our goals. It was Jay's vision and brilliance that was the true leader. My role was to do whatever I could to hire and retain a team and create an environment for success. There was no playbook to follow, as this was 1996 in Stamford, Connecticut. But we hired amazing, passionate professionals of all ages and backgrounds. We often paired a twenty-three-year-old college grad with Internet experience with a forty- or fifty-year-old airline executive who shared the same passion for the solution that Priceline would provide consumers and airlines. It was amazing, and many of those friendships are still in place, working on other projects both commercial and philanthropic. How cool is that!

Regarding his leadership, Jesse said that he is "rarely the smartest in the room, and if I am, I don't want to be there." He always tries to fill the room with smart, passionate people.

Jesse and Betsy faced a major change in their lives when Priceline went public in 2001. They felt overwhelmed by the sudden wealth. They knew immediately that they wanted to give back, and they studied what other philanthropic families had done. The two had met at the State University of New York (SUNY) in its College of Environmental Science and Forestry and were committed to environmental issues. They focused on funding to solve environmental challenges, particularly in climate change. In 2001, they formed the Betsy and Jesse Fink Foundation for "catalytic environmental and educational grant making."

Although they fund in the area of environmental issues, it is really about the people. After an exhaustive analysis early in their foundation's history, the team concluded that investing in climate through both investments and grants would have the most impact. Jesse and Betsy have led the holistic process internally since 2004 to inspire their team and their peers to be catalytic in the transition to a low-carbon economy.

With two expert investment partners, Jesse, the entrepreneur, established MissionPoint Capital Partners, a private investment firm focused on energy and the environment. In 2007, he raised $335 million with a community of principals of like-minded investment firms who wanted financial return and impact creation.

After the United Nations Climate Change Conference in 2009 in Copenhagen and the failure of the United States to ratify the Kyoto Protocol, which bound countries to reduce greenhouse gas emissions, three issues stood out for Betsy and Jesse:

1. The environmental problems are so large that it would be hard to know they were making a difference.

2. Success for transformative action is more likely at the local and regional levels, and concentrating their leadership closer to home could be more effective.

3. By touching the lives of individuals and supporting their learning from one another, perhaps they could make a difference.

Another dimension of genuine leadership is knowing your purpose. Jesse and Betsy, through their twelve years of philanthropic giving, have now paid more attention to environmental leadership. Although they had often funded internships for young people in nonprofit organizations, the pattern was reactive funding. In 2012, they decided to be more strategic in the process by focusing on three specific geographies—with a defined theme. "We have focused on Northeast agriculture and food systems," said Jesse, "because we see it and feel it locally, and it is a key sector that brings together many of today's most pressing problems, including climate change, but also water, land use, and food access, and healthy eating and childhood obesity."

Betsy's vision for creating Millstone Farm in Wilton, Connecticut, has enabled them to understand gaps and barriers in the food systems sector, an understanding that can guide their grant making and investments. Millstone Farm uses sustainable agriculture to cultivate local, regional, and global communities. It's a working farm serving as an educational outreach hub, supporting other farmers, community organizations, school groups, and restaurateurs who are interested in learning more about the practice of sustainable agriculture, its implementation, and its impact on food quality and local economies.

As Betsy and Jesse became more focused and realized that they as entrepreneurs continue to inspire social entrepreneurs in the philanthropic sector and beyond, they have expanded their venture philanthropy. Integrating a philosophy of layering investment in human capital for small start-up nonprofits or innovative initiatives within larger organizations, and then providing their knowledge and expertise to inspire and give guidance, has ignited a strategy to create impact for an aspiring next generation of leaders.

Betsy and Jesse have been referred to as patrons in the old sense of the word. They have a keen sense of identifying younger organizations that provide a niche. Betsy and Jesse provide funding for interns and fellows to help create the next generation of environmental leaders. "That is exciting to us," said Jesse. "We see the network of people whose lives we are changing."

Jesse reported meeting with a coach last year, and from that work he took three words that symbolized what he and Betsy do: *inspire, empower,* and *connect.* "We do this in all aspects of our lives," he said. "If we find someone of worth in whom to invest, we can inspire them and then connect them to others."

Genuine leaders also take risks. Betsy and Jesse are involved in local and regional start-ups and in innovative programs in larger organizations. They have chosen not to be on many boards. And with risking comes failures. Jesse said, "If you haven't failed, you haven't learned." They failed often, but they learned from their failures. They realize that risk taking is part of their leadership.

Jesse and Betsy have discovered that traditional grant making won't solve the huge environmental problems. They work with an investment model that is sometimes more effective. Currently, they are exploring an exercise of creating a policy around investment goals, and they are presenting their ideas to some high-net-worth colleagues, admitting it is a work in progress. For example, if wealth holders can afford an "Impact Portfolio"—meaning if they lost the money, it would not change their lives—they could take more risks with impact investing. Jesse admits that working with impact investing is complicated. Yet he knows that financial returns are not enough. There is a large group of investors who, in addition to the financial return, also are tied to a psychological return, and this is related to impact. Impact investing is less measure-focused. Jesse and Betsy want to be catalysts. They check to see whether, if they made an investment, others followed. "If indeed we plugged the gap, the risk goes down," Jesse explained. He is enthusiastic that "if other high-net-worth families see us as an example on how to tie passion and purpose to all their activities, the returns will be multiplied on many levels."

Recently some of their philanthropy has been supporting documentary films. Whether concerning climate change or food-related issues, the Finks believe that messengers play a key role, and they have actively guided the filmmakers and scientists to strategize content and outreach. Jesse believes attracting the next generation to be aware and involved in these issues is critical. Together the Finks are helping to fund a film on childhood obesity.

Jesse notes that when he and Betsy take a group skiing, they lead together in the same way they lead in their philanthropy. One may take the lead upfront for a while and, at another time, lead from behind.

People trust the Finks. "Our rawness of who we are, our authenticity, can be inspiring," Jesse admits. They know that when what they are doing is right for the planet and people, they can inspire, and they can be discerning in leveraging the network in which they live. Jesse sums up their leadership this way: "It's like the old model car—you have your foot on the gas and the clutch, and that is how we lead."

When I reflect on the genuine leadership of Jesse and Betsy Fink, I am reminded of what one high-level leader said of them: "They do so much good work without pretense or vanity." This is perhaps the highest compliment any leader could aspire to.

Pathways for Change

In this exercise, you will use the Model of Family and Company Culture to assess your family and workplace culture. The model shows four quadrants. Review the four quadrant descriptions before you begin your assessment.

Family and Work Culture Assessment

The ability of every employee can be strengthened by the organization's work culture. Retired Costco CEO Jim Sinegal has said, "Culture is not just an important thing; it is the *only* thing."

Your challenge is to examine the work culture you have entered and ask, "What behaviors might I be bringing to the workplace that mirror some of the patterns I learned from my parents and first family?"

Begin by exploring your first family. Where would you place it among the four quadrants? Then assess your workplace. What are the similarities between your family and your workplace? What are the differences? Did you find your family at work? Or did you choose well and find the same healthy system in which you grew up? Knowing the rules from home can help to change the rules at work.

Notice how the change arrow intersects all four quadrants. You can see how change can evolve into transformation when the arrow moves to the left quadrants. When you identify where you have lived and where you work, you can more clearly see that there is a way through to the Vital quadrant.

Overtly Disabling Quadrant

Quadrant 1, the Overtly Disabling quadrant, refers to the behaviors that have led to the awakening crisis or "wake-up call"—whether externally or internally driven. This is the time of facing and naming the behavior, the actions that have brought the disabling behaviors to surface—the call to change. The behaviors representative of quadrant

Model of Family and Company Culture

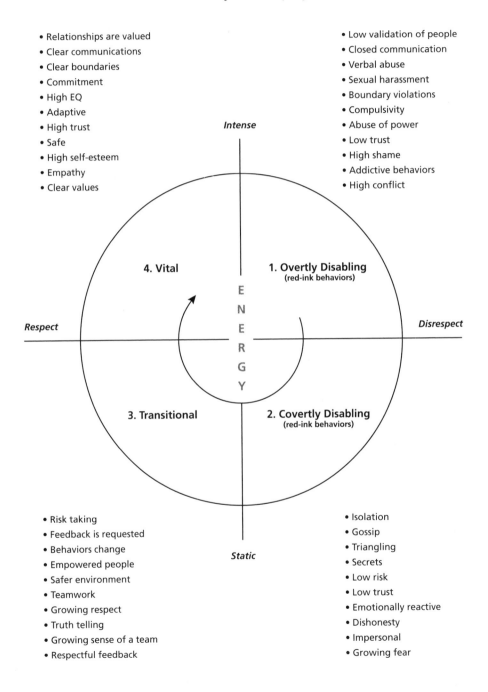

1 lie at the far end of the continuum with disrespect and high intensity. This quadrant frames the behaviors that keep the system stuck.

Characteristics of the Overtly Disabling quadrant are high fear, low trust, verbal abuse, sexual harassment, intimidation, compulsive behaviors, boundary violations, high emotional reactivity, and the no-talk rule.

Most leadership teams do not plan to create dynamics that operate from abusive power, nor do they intend to use shunning and isolation to remove someone from their ranks. They merely act out what has become normalized in their workplace, often smoothed over with a tacit veneer of acceptance. "Red-ink" behaviors—such as high-level complaints, lack of cooperation, and insincere "act as if" behaviors— are prevalent here, costing companies unimaginable costs.

Covertly Disabling Quadrant

Quadrant 2, the Covertly Disabling quadrant, shows a less intense energy or reactivity charge, yet the behaviors still fall at the disrespectful end of the continuum. This is also an area where we see red-ink behaviors.

Characteristics of the Covertly Disabling quadrant behaviors are sarcasm, cynicism, emotional dishonesty, secrets, silence, ostracizing, low risk taking, emotional abuse, isolation, buried pain, gossip, and "triangling," which is talking to one person about another or bringing an outsider's view into discussions.

Transitional Quadrant

Quadrant 3, the Transitional quadrant, shows movement in the direction of increased respect. This is the area of modifying behaviors with a commitment toward real change. As new skills are learned and implemented, people in this culture have increased optimism and a sense of team.

The characteristics of the Transitional quadrant are growing respect for "team" and "we," increased expression of feelings, increased honest feedback, and changes in behaviors and attitudes.

The Dynamic, Robust, Vital System

The move into quadrant 4, Vital system, involves something of a leap into the unknown. This is the stage in which leaders are willing to experiment with new practices and to make mistakes. A true sense of "we" exists within the organization.

The characteristics of the Vital quadrant are high EQ that permits empathy before strategy and allows feelings to be expressed, a management philosophy of equal concern for human and fiscal assets, an attitude of deep respect that creates an emotionally safe workplace, and implicit rules for interaction with respect for boundaries that create a high level of trust. In addition, the highly spirited system recognizes that relationship skills are a valued component of business. Finally, there is acknowledgment of differences. Gender, race, and class diversity are welcomed.

7

When Home Values Are Company Values

[KEEPING IT IN THE FAMILY]

"Of all the rocks upon which we build our lives,
we are reminded today that family is the most important."
— BARACK OBAMA, FORTY-FOURTH PRESIDENT OF THE UNITED STATES

One of the many positive indicators of a living company is that values once taught in the home are being taught at work. Businesses now teach how to fight fairly (conflict resolution) and how to develop group or "family cooperation" through team building. Respect is taught through diversity- and gender-awareness workshops. In fact, many employees report that the workplace has become a place of civility and manners—while home often remains a site of dissension. While differences were being addressed and resolved at work, at home the fights dragged on. Some researchers found that the preference to be at work over home was so strong that even young parents did not step forward when flexible schedule options were offered to employees.[1] Still, more than 37 percent of employees report that they take their stress from the office home with them.

For many companies, though, the solution is to make families feel included in the company, either as corporate policy, or literally when it's the family running the business. We'll look at a corporate leader, Rick Schnieders, and then at an entrepreneurial couple, Steve and Barb King, whose family values were essential to their success. We'll then explore three family-owned businesses to see how, when family systems are brought into the workplace, they become the company family system, and how facing the dysfunction in one can transform the other.

The Heart of the Matter:
When Family Values and Business Values Coincide

One thing that has surprised me in my consulting work is that I have felt forced to create codes of conduct for many companies' senior-management teams. One would hardly think that would be necessary for these well-educated, high-paid, well-dressed executives. But proper conduct was not "natural" for those whose family values did not include honesty, generosity, and empathy.

Of course, not all leaders come from dysfunctional families. Many people learn the values of trust, integrity, and loyalty at their parents' knees. They grow up to be employers and employees who work hard, treat their colleagues respectfully, and are willing to go the distance when needed. Companies with this type of leaders have the edge on becoming a living company. Proper conduct was indeed natural for retired CEO and board chair Rick Schnieders. The same can be said for Steve and Barb King, two entrepreneurs whose commitment and perseverance revolutionized how children play around the world. Let's look at their stories.

Rick's Story

Rick Schnieders, former CEO and board chair of Sysco Corporation, the largest food-distribution company in North America, is an example of a person who internalized positive messages. His loyalty served him in a most positive way. Rick grew up in a German Catholic family in a small Iowa town. He was the firstborn of five children, working three hours a day after school and all day on Saturdays in his father's grocery store. (Today, his father would be considered an entrepreneur, branching out from groceries to start a greenhouse, a flower shop, and a small slaughterhouse.)

When Rick left to study math at the University of Iowa, he told his dad, "I will never work in food again." Then after his college graduation in 1970, he went to work for the Supervalu Inc. grocery store chain! Rick continued to live his family's message: "Do the best you can at whatever you are doing." Rick moved from cutting meat to human relations, then to management.

When he entered a training program with Sysco in 1982, he was allowed to work in all departments of the company. When Rick left in 2009 after serving as CEO and board chair, Sysco Corporation had 140 acquisitions with revenue of $37 billion.

When I asked Rick about his use of consultants in creating his company's culture, he stared and in silence. "Well, I really did not use consultants, other than a coach for myself for a while," he admitted. Rick took over as board chair in 2003 and made changes in the board's structure; the only consultant hired was for strategic planning. The employee retention at the firm was 98 percent. Spouses were encouraged to "join" the system. Rick's wife frequently traveled with him. When I asked him about what accounted for his success in leading a company, he recounted, "Well, I was from the Midwest; I had learned to listen." After reading *Quiet*,[2] Susan Cain's book about the power of introverts, I would give Rick the label of a Reflective Leader. I would add that Rick is a most respectful human being, a leader who did not need to clamor to get to the top. His work success evolved from being motivated by living the values of his Midwestern family's rules. Rick's focus on family and the impact of work on the family's overall well-being was the result of these values.

Rick knew that the workplace has power over families' lives. When family members are treated with respect, they will be able and willing to support the corporation. Often when interviewing company leaders, I ask the question, "Have you ever counted the total number of people who are dependent on your decisions—outside your individual employees? Their families? Your communities?" Most often the interviewees initially present a blank expression, followed by the answer, "Well, no, I guess I never figured that." It always brings a stop to our conversation as the realization sinks in that they indeed have real influence at many levels.

For years, professionals have attempted to change family systems by working with the family members (or whole families) one at a time. This approach ignores the power that corporations hold over family life. When those "other parents"—corporate management—make decisions, they have far more wide-reaching effects on families, both positive and negative, than do other professionals' (such as counselors and communication programs) efforts to work with families and individuals. In today's changing world, we see the impact of the *context* of where we are working.

Entrepreneurship and Sharing the Risk—and the Success: Steve and Barb

For some, finding the genuine leader within themselves comes from a spirit of entrepreneurship, creative thinking, and plain hard work. Steve King, the founder of Landscape Structures, is truly a genuine leader. Steve and his wife, Barb, founded Landscape Structures in 1971. Today the company is one of the leading public playground equipment manufacturers in the world, supplying more than seventy-five thousand playgrounds worldwide. Although they are highly successful today, Steve and Barb spent years sacrificing in many ways to achieve the success of their award-winning company.

The story began when Steve, a student at Iowa State University's landscape architecture department, chose to design a playground as part of a larger project. When Steve observed children in parks, waiting in line to use a slide or swings, he saw that they didn't seem very happy. In contrast, when he visited the university's child development department, he saw kids playing follow the leader, making their own games, making their own spaces—for instance, inside cardboard boxes—and manipulating things, even in sand play. He saw that, when children had the freedom to develop their own space, they also created their own games and challenges. Steve observed that children responded to play that had a continuous flow; he also saw that when they had discontinuous elements, like a swing or a slide, not many could play at one time.

He got the idea to plan structures that could enable children to play together in a variety of challenges, moving from one activity to another, without touching the ground. This is what he came later to call the "continuous play concept." Little did he realize that he was giving birth to a new concept.

At the review of his project in the landscape architecture department, he was told his concept of continuous play within the open space of a townhouse development would not work. In fact, his professor gave him a C+ on his project, which was devastating to Steve—but also motivating. Today his structures using the continuous play concept are at parks, schools, child-care centers, theme parks, and places of worship around the world.

When I asked Steve about his early childhood, he said that as a boy he always wanted something to do and couldn't sit still. He would ask, "What can I do?" "Just that energy is what started me thinking life doesn't have to be what I see around me," he said. His folks were not that creative; his father was a preacher. He said he felt his own personality came out when he was busy in the outdoors. For him a degree in landscape architecture was a natural fit—it combined both creativity and the outdoors.

Steve's leadership began when he was elected president of his high school senior class. After college, Steve married Barb, who was to become not only his life partner but also his business partner for the next forty years. After working for a local site-planning firm for nearly two years, he left to start his own company. During those two years, he was able to build the first play structure featuring the continuous play concept. It was very successful and started a revolution.

Barb had a job as a home economist at The Pillsbury Company when Steve started the company at their home, and she also worked part-time with him to build a successful playground manufacturing business. Although his business was respected and desired, the early years were very difficult. Steve said that they had to foreclose on their home five times. He commonly worked sixteen- to eighteen-hour days seven days a week. They ate two meals a day and sold most of their furniture at yard sales. On top of that, Barb's department at Pillsbury closed, and a month later she announced she was pregnant.

145

Then the city of Minneapolis asked them to stop manufacturing playgrounds at their home. They had to find a new place to do business. After being asked to leave three different warehouse spaces, they finally found a permanent home in Delano, Minnesota, in 1981.

The story of Landscape Structures' start is a classic case of having a lot of opportunities but no means to exploit them. In the early years, they had no credit; they had to pay cash for everything. This meant they could only build one play structure at a time. They had no employees. In short, they had to take the phone off the hook. They had borrowed $1,000 to start the business, then got two Small Business Administration (SBA) loans. They were down to their last fifty cents when, after a lot of soul searching, they made the decision to forge ahead with their entrepreneurial dream. This meant finding money to allow them to grow. Within a couple of weeks, a leader from the Young President's Organization heard Steve's story, and along with his peers, gave Steve and Barb $40,000 in exchange for 50 percent of the company. Now they were off and running. From there it was a steady, uphill climb. In 1990, they bought their stock back from the investors.

In their work as a team, Steve said he was referred to as the "hardware," responsible for thirty employees, and Barb was known as the "software," the cultural icon of the company, with 275 employees ranging from manufacturing plant workers to office staff reporting to her. They grew their company as they grew in their industry and won many awards for environmental stewardship, safety, best business practices, and one of the best places to work in Minnesota. In 1992, Ernst and Young, *Inc. Magazine,* and the law firm of Gray Plant Mooty named them Entrepreneurs of the Year in Minnesota, and in 1994, the SBA named Barb the Small Business Person of the Year in the Midwest region.

Landscape Structures moved from working with wood to aluminum to plastics and then to concrete. Today the company uses a variety of materials, many of which have a high recycled content. They sell more than two thousand products to a variety of customers through independent sales representatives. In addition, Steve has developed playgrounds for children with disabilities and outdoor equipment for seniors.

Barb started the Säjai Foundation to help prevent the rapid growth of childhood obesity. At Iowa State University, the Kings set up the Barbara A. King Scholarship Endowment for Innovation and Entrepreneurship scholarships. When Barb died of cancer in 2008, more than one thousand people attended her memorial service. In 2010, the Barb King Inspiration Park, a one-of-a-kind playground, was built in their hometown of Delano, Minnesota, in her memory. Today Steve has moved his creativity to a village in Zambia, Africa, where he is building community play equipment with local wood to help local villagers become self-sufficient and self-sustaining. He also helped to build a play structure there, where kids have a chance to experience the continuous play concept.

When I asked Steve how he thought his employees would describe him, he paused. He said, "Perhaps [as] an idea guy who will listen to any ideas—energetic, open, honest, available." Steve does not micromanage. When you meet Steve, you quickly see that "who you see is who you get," an apt descriptor of a genuine leader.

Aptly, Steve believes in humor and play in the workplace. In a TV profile, Landscape Structures employees were shown outside at "recess," a time to take a break and play! He explained that the company's human resources department acts proactively in assuring employee health and welfare.

As I write this, Steve is no longer head of his forty-three-year-old company. When outsiders wanted to buy the company, with its three hundred employees and sales of more than $100 million in a campus of six buildings, Steve and Barb realized that they had plenty of money. They decided to turn their company over to their employees as part of their estate planning. In 2004, they set up an employee stock ownership plan (ESOP), and by the end of 2012, the employees owned 100 percent of the company. Steve's only role now is as chair of the board. Steve and Barb King have truly created a legacy; their story is told in his inspiring book *A Legacy of Play*.

Genuine Leaders and ESOPS

ESOPs began in the mid-nineteenth century with the rise of industrialization. When Richard Sears and Alvah Curtis Roebuck, as well as William Procter and James Gamble, recognized that some of their employees could work for the companies for twenty-plus years and reach old age with no retirement income, they began setting aside stock that could be cashed in upon retirement. In the early twentieth century, the growth of ESOPs was well on its way. Many companies have partial employee ownership; many have full employee ownership in the style of Landscape Structures. For example, many people do not realize that W. W. Norton & Company publishers, Eileen Fisher fashions, United Airlines, and Avis Car Rental are (or were at one time) either partially or fully owned by their employees.

Today, more than ten million employees participate in more than eleven thousand ESOP plans. Overall, employees now control about 8 percent of corporate equity. A recent study showed that S corporations (ESOPs) added jobs more quickly than other companies over the past decade. The strategies of genuine leaders are bringing forth win-wins for their employees and their companies.

The Family Business

"There's a lot of pride and a lot of passion put into a family business that has survived as long as ours. This is a labor of love."

— LEE SCHWEBEL, DIRECTOR OF MARKETING AT
SCHWEBEL BAKING COMPANY, FOUNDED BY HIS GREAT-GRANDPARENTS,
JOSEPH AND DORA SCHWEBEL, IN 1906 IN YOUNGSTOWN, OHIO

Almost 70 percent of all new businesses in the United States are established in homes or home offices and employ the founder of the business and perhaps one or two other people. The trends today indicate that within the next fifteen years, there will be one company for every three workers! It's amazing that companies with fewer than twenty individuals are responsible for about 90 percent of new-work job creation. Of course, many of these workers are not salaried and are part-time or temporary.

Many business writers have stated that the twentieth century was the first and last century in which most people were salaried. Until the last decades of the nineteenth century, most people were self-employed farmers, artisans, storekeepers, and such. It now appears that by the middle of the twenty-first century, most people will again be self-employed. In recent years, we have seen the growth of what are called "portfolio workers," who have skills in several different areas—predicted by many to be the fastest-growing class in the work market. Many studies suggest that young people entering the work market today will have between five to seven careers in their lifetimes and fifteen to twenty places of work. The traits of flexibility and the ability to learn new skills are what will be sought moving forward.

Often people running family businesses also exhibit such flexibility and learning abilities, especially if the business is small or starting up and each family member involved wears several "hats." Today 65 percent of U.S. businesses are family businesses, constituting 60 percent of the labor force and generating 50 percent of our gross national product (GNP). In addition, family businesses represent approximately 37 percent of *Fortune* 500 businesses.[3]

But family businesses face some of the greatest changes of all. Through their inherited legacies, which are alive and well in the boardroom and in the family members' various roles, these businesses often appear to be immune to change. We often refer to the founders as "ruling from the grave," coming from deep family roots. Based on the studies that find most companies run about ten years and most corporations about forty, it follows that many family businesses will only last for one or two generations, yet their inherited patterns are passed on and often controlled by the seniors in the family.

As we saw in the story of the West Coast fifth-generation family business of John and Sue in chapter 2, dynamics can change when a disabling factor such as alcoholism arises in the family culture. Often a process of family intervention can move a stuck organization into a robust, healthy organization.

Ken

Dynamics can also change in a positive way when a courageous family business owner who is very thoughtful about succession planning leads the business in a way that keeps it alive for the next generation. I recall seeing the surprise in the audience when Ken, the retiring CEO of his Midwestern family business, announced that he had established a policy for his two sons whereby they had to work outside of the family business for a minimum of five years before entering the family enterprise.

Both did find work on Wall Street, and both later gave up their lucrative jobs to return to the family business. When they came back, Ken moved his office across town, because he knew of the power of his multiyear leadership in the firm. His sons could truly "come of age" in the business without their father's influence.

Erik and Sandra

Often family businesses do not work smoothly, especially when the issue of succession arises. Sandra and Erik Smith had started a small family enterprise in the Midwest that grew very successfully; it did not take long before the three children had roles in the company. Known for their business's high-quality window and door products, the Smiths had called me in because of their goal—"to turn it over." The senior Smiths were adamant: "If we don't do it together, then no one gets it." Sandra and Erik had a mutual goal—that their children would continue the legacy. "But," Sandra said quietly, "we cannot see the children working together—they simply are not aligned."

They had clearly named one key problem: the children and their spouses. Sandra and Erik had one son and two daughters. Jim, the son, and his family had moved to California to be away from the Smith family, yet he longed to return to his Midwestern roots and someday take over the business. He was a political progressive—the only one in the family. He knew the industry well and enjoyed taking risks. His wife, Nancy, was glad to live away from the family and "all those family rituals the folks seemed to enjoy so much." The two daughters and their husbands lived nearby. Marie's husband, Joe, had been out of work for a period of time, so Sandra and Erik had offered him the job of general manager, a role he now held. Paul, married to the Smiths' daughter Cynthia, had the advertising contract for the business. He had a strong marketing background and was often at odds with Joe regarding their strategic planning and marketing ideas.

When I came into the family meeting, it was soon obvious that founder's syndrome was alive and well. What Sandra and Erik said they wanted—succession plans—was stated clearly, but when I interviewed each of the couples and individuals separately, I learned quickly that Sandra had tight control. Erik, an easygoing man, who wanted to lead quietly at Sandra's side, revealed that their names (both his and Sandra's) were on all the documents. Sandra, in their family board meeting, held great veto power (even though she and Erik were not official board members). Erik said it was difficult to walk what seemed like a tightrope; he did not know which hat to wear—his hard-core business hat or his soft, kindly family hat.

As the family talked openly and heard one another's concerns, values, and desires, they faced their trust issues. I heard a wide range of results when I asked each of them to describe their family business as a car (an exercise that you'll find in the Pathways for Change section at this chapter's end). First I asked them to choose the model and make of the car, its year, and the color. Next I asked them to state what the car was doing, what was happening. Was the car parked or moving, and who was driving? Some of the family members described the business as an old car chugging along; others considered it a solid, well-built truck. When they responded about who was in the driver's seat, they saw a group disagreeing about who should drive. Several agreed it needed a new engine. As the family members heard their differing responses, they began to laugh at themselves and recognize how different their perceptions were. This rather simple exercise presented a safety net—another way for them to recognize their differences and to see their family business and their roles in it.

Eventually Joe admitted that he was not really suited for the general manager job and that it was causing great stress in his marriage.

He and Marie finally admitted the stress was not worth the costs. Jim and Nancy decided that they would risk moving back to the Midwest and taking charge of the home office; Jim could work closely with his father in learning the financial side of the business. Since Jim and his brother-in-law Paul had a good working relationship, Paul was able to stay on with the title of marketing director. At my suggestion, after working with a family business attorney, the documents were drawn up with equal ownership shares for the three siblings' families. As the next generation took over ownership, Erik and Sandra stopped coming to family meetings for a long time. Eventually they were welcome to participate in the meetings as nonvoting board members.

Carlos

When I introduced Carlos to the Model of Family and Company Culture (discussed in the previous chapter's Pathways for Change section), he and his executive committee identified themselves in the Covertly Disabling quadrant. They acknowledged that fear, secrets, and mistrust drove the system and that emotional dishonesty was normalized among their entire senior-management team. Their firm, an established vending-machine company, was several generations old when I was called in to work with its team.

In our first conference call, five family members who ran the company phoned in from various areas of the country. Immediately I felt overwhelmed; they all talked over one another. Several made snide, rude remarks. I was shocked to witness such behavior when they were creating a first impression with their potential consultant. Hearing the dynamics in the family group, I said that I could not work with their enterprise at all until I did a few "offsite" premeetings with some of the key players. I flew to the West Coast to meet with two different sets of the company's leadership. What I learned there was most revealing—all the children had vied for their father's attention. Their family had come to the United States from Mexico, where their great-great-grandfather, a leading wealthy industrialist, had started the family business and dedicated his life to his career in the family business. Carlos said, sadly, "The only time I remember my father touching me was when he held my hand walking to Mass on Sunday mornings." Others reported on their father's psychological absence. When he *did* show up for family dinners, he was totally preoccupied with his business affairs and never inquired about the children's lives.

Carlos and his cousin described how competitive they had been for leadership positions as they entered the family enterprise. When I met with the two sisters who were part of the executive team, they told about their childhood resentments, because their mother had favored the sister who had had polio as a child. I asked to meet with them as a family before we went inside the business; they had never spoken together in a safe environment about their history. In a long family history retreat, secrets were revealed, resentments were owned, and losses acknowledged. Carlos, his siblings, and his cousins also spoke about their experience in private schools here in America and feeling like outsiders when taunted about their darker skin color. The team could clearly see that their dysfunctional team behavior was born from their shadowed past. There was genuine warmth in the room after they individually revealed their truths to one another. I saw then that we could start to work. I brought in a family trust attorney to work with me; the total family enterprise consisted of thirty-six people. Some family members were feeling hostile about some of their cousins managing their trusts. There were also classism issues in the family, which were born from their varied educational levels.

We began our work with family members participating in creating a code of conduct regarding their behavioral expectations. They displayed these "rules" at every meeting. Over time we moved through the Model of Family and Company Culture's four quadrants. They realized it was not enough to analyze their culture; they needed tools for change. By using the tools provided by the Model of Family and Company Culture (reluctantly at first), they gradually saw positive change in their dynamics. They were very successful personally and professionally in advancing from what began as cultural change to cultural transformation. About ten months after we terminated our work, I received a CD in the mail from Carlos. He and the team were so proud of their new behaviors, they had decided I should have a recording of their last meeting—a meeting illustrating a culture of respect! I smiled both outwardly and inwardly. This was indeed the real "payment" for my work and the family members' work—witnessing the attitude changes that they'd achieved.

As leaders make changes in their organizations, could they not make changes in *all* systems, bringing the same new tools from the workplace into their homes and communities? It is challenging to think of how U.S. companies could emulate businesses with family values at the core to become living companies and affect the overall standard of living in what many see as a declining empire. Those in the executive suites could take the lead in providing the solid foundation that all cultures need for survival. Doing so would not only foster the greater good of the United States but also would be a positive influence in the global marketplace as well.

Pathways for Change

This section contains a family dynamics questionnaire and the car metaphor exercise. Together they provide useful tools for further exploring the ideas from this chapter.

Family Dynamics Questionnaire

Please rank the following items, using the values indicated:

Strongly Disagree–0; Disagree–1; Slightly Disagree–2; Slightly Agree–3; Agree–4; Strongly Agree–5

	Negative					Positive
We disagree respectfully.	0	1	2	3	4	5
Family members don't hold grudges.	0	1	2	3	4	5
Family politics do not interfere with decision making.	0	1	2	3	4	5
Family members keep commitments.	0	1	2	3	4	5
We are good listeners.	0	1	2	3	4	5
Family members talk directly with one another.	0	1	2	3	4	5
I feel supported by most of my family members.	0	1	2	3	4	5
Our family honors one another.	0	1	2	3	4	5
We have inherited enriching family rituals.	0	1	2	3	4	5
Our family has a sense of humor.	0	1	2	3	4	5
Our family works toward gender balance in family leadership.	0	1	2	3	4	5
Our family works well together.	0	1	2	3	4	5
Family members participate fully in making decisions.	0	1	2	3	4	5

Continued on next page.

Family members are team-oriented.	0	1	2	3	4	5
Family members appreciate differing inputs.	0	1	2	3	4	5
Our family can take critical feedback well.	0	1	2	3	4	5
Our family members give critical feedback well.	0	1	2	3	4	5

Family members have used this questionnaire in a variety of ways. Everyone fills out the questionnaire individually. Some family members may then choose to discuss their "discovered" strengths, followed by their "growing edges" (i.e., areas for improvement). Many family members choose to gather all scores and see how they rate themselves as a group. Often family members choose to make commitments to change and set deadlines for their next follow-up meeting to assess progress.

Metaphor of the Car

1. Describe your business or organization as a car: What model is it? What make? What year? What color?

2. What is the car doing? Is it parked? Is it moving? Where is it?

3. Who is driving the car?

4. What would the car need to proceed most successfully?

This exercise, when used along with the Family Dynamics Questionnaire, is fertile territory for open discussion about how family members' perceptions differ and how they would want to change their perception.

8

Leading from Within
[IGNITING THE SPIRIT AT WORK]

"By choosing integrity, I become more whole,
but wholeness does not mean perfection. It means becoming
more real by using the whole of who I am."

— PARKER PALMER, FOUNDER OF THE CENTER FOR COURAGE & RENEWAL,
AUTHOR OF *LEADING FROM WITHIN* AND OTHER BOOKS

In chapter 6, I mentioned that spiritual flatness is a nationwide malady. It exists in corporations riddled with managers and employees who have low self-esteem, feelings of intimidation, lack of trust, and fear. All the jammed, buried emotional energy from maladaptive dynamics creates a spiritually flat system. The challenge for all of us is to ignite our own spirits. This is what led me to write the book *Igniting the Spirit at Work: Daily Reflections*. Spirituality can be like the flu: some get it, some don't.

Spirituality refers to a person's inner connection with the vital life force that sustains us all. I am not referring to religion, although for some people, spirituality may include a traditional established or a personal religion. For others, it may be a Twelve Step group or a connection with nature. A friend and author, Jo-Anne Krestan, has said, "It doesn't matter what it is, as long as you ain't it."

I confess I was surprised when I heard Deborah Szekely of Rancho La Puerta say she was doing "God's work." The spa offers all kinds of Eastern meditation practices, meditation hikes, and such, but never with any focus on religion in the traditional sense. The spa does, however, have a Shabbat dinner for those who choose to attend. There is also a weekly Twelve Step group meeting.

However, in recent years, spirituality has taken a hold in corporations. Today we see increasing numbers of books written on spirituality in the workplace. The spirituality factor can make the difference in experiencing change and transformation in the corporation. Although there are many spiritual pathways, their core principles are similar. The Twelve Steps of Alcoholics Anonymous provide a time-tested model that has worked with individuals from all backgrounds and beliefs. A universal model like that, which emphasizes humility, compassion, and honesty, can sustain the changes and lead a company from behavioral changes into corporate transformation.

At one Minneapolis firm where I consulted, when employees had struggles—either with senior management or with team members—they would write down the problem and place it in a "God Box." That "box" was actually a folder in a file drawer in one of the secretary's offices that symbolically was their place for letting go. Several of the employees were in Twelve Step groups and found this symbolic folder truly helped them place their distressed emotions to the side.

Perhaps we are indeed entering into what Harvard professor Rosabeth Moss Kanter indicated the United States was in need of: "American Corporate Renaissance," founded in participatory management that allows creativity.[1] Why is the workplace not the place for personal growth? We have long recognized that people grow businesses; why can't we say, "And businesses grow people"?

Richard Barrett's Story

Richard Barrett, assistant to the vice president of the World Bank, decided in the mid-1990s that he either had to leave his position there or make a substantial effort to change the work environment so that he could feel authentic and "take his soul" to work. He put a note on a bulletin board inviting anyone who might be interested in discussing spirit in the workplace to join together over a brown-bag lunch. Initially forty people showed up. Richard learned he was not alone with these feelings. The group grew from 25 to approximately 340 as the meetings continued! This story was reported in the *Washington Post*.[2] Richard was part of a growing group of Americans seeking to bring their "whole selves" to work. After a few years, Richard left to devote his full-time energy to spirituality practices in the workplace. His book *Liberating the Corporate Soul: Building a Visionary Organization*[3] has drawn widespread national and worldwide attention. He has won several awards and today heads the Barrett Values Centre, which provides business professionals with tools and techniques for assessing their values and instilling those positive values that will transform organizations.

The Awakened Spirit

The chapter 2 story of educator Tony Gerlicz is a vivid example of someone who, in the words of Parker Palmer, leads "by word and deed simply because I am here doing what I do." Tony often cites the importance of the work of Parker Palmer, who said that "Authentic leaders aim at liberating the heart, their own and others, so that its powers can liberate the world." This may sound like a tall order, yet through the years, the focus on spirituality in the workplace has gained great ground. There are 500 book titles on spirituality in the workplace. A USA Weekend Poll shows "47% of people say their spirituality was the most important element of their happiness." A 1999 Gallup poll published in *Businessweek* showed that 48% of workers said they talked about their religious faith that day.[4]

Some of the changes being made today in corporate America—such as meditation classes and in-house spirituality groups—can surely lead to awakening the spirit, as long as these changes are solidly based on trust, respect, and emotional safety. Meditation classes are now held at many corporations such as Medtronic, Apple, Google, McKinsey, and Cisco. Tyson Foods and Coca-Cola have part-time chaplains. Today there is a higher awareness than ever that the ego attempts to "buy out" the spirit.

I have found that most large corporations are unwilling to examine their spiritual void—until they are successful enough to allow reflection. Those who are in the middle of their corporate climb may not have enough energy to focus on the spirit at work. Harry Levinson, a psychologist who studied workplace motivation beginning in the 1950s, commented, "They just won't listen!" A crisis, whether a personal emergency or an attempted company takeover, may awaken a management group to the importance of spirit.

We know of many young entrepreneurial leaders who do allow for spirit, creativity, and play in the workplace. This characterizes many of the technology companies that created Silicon Valley and the digital revolution. They are aware of the rate of change we are experiencing and they are facing change creatively.

Focusing on spirit also means looking closely at diversity in the workplace—race, class, gender, and economic diversity. In chapter 4, we talked about how women have come to recognize and confront the discrimination they have faced and continue to face in the workplace. The same can be said for many racial and cultural minorities, who only in the last forty years have begun to make significant headway in gaining equal recognition in corporate America.

Several years ago, I led a seminar for corporate women in which I asked them to tell stories of "finding their voices" and speaking "truth to power." One woman stood tall when she stated that she, as a lesbian, felt put down by some of the comments overheard in her workplace. She had decided to come out at work. Along with some other gay and lesbian employees, she went into the president's office and said that they were going to be known. They also stated that if it were not acceptable, then they would have to leave. They reported that it was difficult enough to live with the glass ceiling, but in addition, they were weary of pretending they were single or fictionalizing their personal lives. To their delight and surprise, the president received the messages openly, created new policies with their help, and instituted benefits policies for same-sex relationships. Not long after that scene, the firm announced its first woman CEO! This, indeed, was a transformation. When we find that place within us where commitment grows and we take stands, the rest of the world can respond respectfully. I like to think of this as spirit at work.

No matter where we are placed within an organization, the challenge for all of us is to ignite our own spirits. What are the signs of an ignited spirit? First, people need to care about each other as equals and commit to making their company a place that's welcoming for anyone who is committed to creating a living company where employees find purpose and meaning. Second, work can be a major source of self-esteem and personal growth. When spirits are ignited at work, we see the opening of hearts, expression of feelings, and respect for one another.

Alex von Bidder's Story

Alex von Bidder, co-owner of The Four Seasons Restaurant in New York City, exemplifies what it means to be an ignited spirit. His courage in facing his shadow has made a real difference in his ability to provide genuine leadership.

Alex was the first son and the middle child in a family of three children with a manic-depressive father. Their mother was the family's driver. She had to make the financial decisions and be the taskmaster. Even though Alex came to see his father as emotionally available and was able to enjoy his friendship, he didn't see him as the model for what he wanted to achieve in life.

Alex reported that his first leadership lesson was as a Scout leader when he led a troop in Switzerland. In Switzerland's scout troops, the boys led the boys. Alex was fourteen when he led his first troop of ten or twelve boys. They also had leadership training weekends led by the sixteen- and seventeen-year-olds. He said he heard one message that clung to him: "'You only lead people if you care for them.' It surprised me and it stuck with me."

Alex said, "To bring spirit to work is to recognize that it is there already. I'm not bringing anything but myself. When I trust the spirit, then I approach it with the right attitude, knowing that I am part of all this, and all this is part of me."

At age forty-three, at the advice of colleague, magazine editor, and communications consultant T. George Harris, Alex took a ManKind

Project training and found what it was like to be held accountable. He said it was the most significant moment in his life, a situation in which he could safely come to terms with his shadow. He was able to open up and learn that other men have similar struggles. He worked with the others there on facing their shame stories, and he faced his feelings of "never good enough." He found that he "medicated" his shame by seeking perfection, but he also found that "It kills the soul." At the end of the weekend, Alex was transformed and went on to become a leader in the ManKind Project, where he still leads seminars. He realized his mission was to inspire transformation by helping people face their shadows by working together to cocreate "safety, beauty, and joy."

When talking about his leadership, he said he has learned that it only takes 2 or 3 percent of people to influence the outcome in an organization through inner work, through ongoing consciousness development. "I have a group of Buddhist men working with me—waiters and cooks—who have an inner practice," he said. "We are convinced it has a positive effect on the workforce. My tie to Buddhism [became a real] gift when the Dalai Lama visited The Four Seasons." As Alex was leading the way out, the Dalai Lama grabbed his arm and, arm in arm, they walked out together, giggling joyously all the way.

Alex said he was very proud of his record with his 140 employees, of whom 120 are union members. He tells of a recent time when the outgoing union agent came by to introduce his successor to the crew. Alex walked by and tapped the union leader on the shoulder. The union head saw that it was Alex, and they hugged one another. The union leader told his successor, "This is an employer we never ever fought with. We had differences, but we never fought."

Alex faced a challenge, as did many others in the New York City area, after 9/11. The world had fallen apart for many on that day, and a lot of people were in distress and panic. Alex recalled, "I was able to see beyond that day and trust that all is well and all will be well." He continued, "I trusted whatever came to me was the right thing to say and to do. I left it up to the individuals to do what they wanted to do, and I said that our job remains the same—we have to be open and serve lunch for our customers, whether they come or not." One of his long-term employees later said, "Alex, you could have been my pastor."

In addition to running The Four Seasons, Alex was named one of the best male yoga instructors in the New York area in the March 2012 issue of *Esquire* magazine.

Throughout this book, we've seen many leaders who, like Alex, can project a light that allows bursts of new growth in their companies. We also have seen that others cast a shadow under which seedlings die. All too often, leaders fail because they have not been willing to walk into their own shadows. Ignoring of the shadow eventually erupts in the headline-making stories of corruption and greed that we read about daily. A genuine leader is one who casts a bright light.

Max's Spiritual Journey

Satisfied with his income and his consulting firm's growth, Max realized something was missing, even though he had made the dream of his college years come true—to own his own business at age thirty-two. Initially, he had planned with his marketing whiz partner to grow the business to eighteen employees, but they soon realized they were on a growth curve. After only three years, they now had forty-two people working for them.

Yet suddenly Max faced a crisis from within. It began with an internal monologue. "I am without another dream. What is my purpose? Why am I doing this?" he asked himself. "I'm healthy, happily married, with a six-year-old daughter and a four-year-old son—plenty of money . . . why do I not feel satisfied?" Max stopped working in the company on a day-to-day basis and continued to wonder: "Why am I doing what I am doing? I am lost."

This inner crisis led Max to a personal-growth workshop, where he learned that he had been acting a professional role or persona he thought was necessary to be successful, but that he knew all along it was a facade rather than "being really me." He also knew the facade had worked for him, making him successful in material terms, but that something was missing. In the early 1990s, Max went on the journey to find out why he did what he did.

During this period, Max awoke one night, very troubled. With no clothes on, he stood before a full-length mirror and began to talk with himself. "That's all you are. What are you all about? What is the truth of that persona versus who you really are?" Max faced his true nakedness, inwardly and outwardly.

He hired a spiritual coach from whom he learned the power of visualization and imagery and explored in depth the family in which he'd grown up. Through this journey inward, he said, "I think I learned to trust people to a certain level and to be in relationships. How to trust the rest of me with others was the issue. I have to be me in all of this." He explored the meaning of genuine leadership through facing his vulnerability. Gradually he could say from within, "This is what I am doing. This is my purpose. I learned you cannot find out without first going in, so I went in fully!"

Max soon found his new insights put to the test; he was out of town and his partner called to tell him that the person they were bringing into the partnership did not want to sign the contract with the terms Max had offered. Typically, Max would have told him that he had to sign it, and if he didn't, his partner would be in trouble. Instead, Max heard himself asking his partner, "What do you think?" His partner told him how he would handle it, which was not at all what Max would have done. Max then heard himself say, "Since I am not there, you decide. Whatever you do is okay."

Max said this was a first for him; he broke his own rule and put the decision in his partner's hands. For the first time in his life, he was willing to go with the consequences. He was beginning to trust—to trust his own decisions and to trust his partner. "From around age two, I had been doing it all myself," Max said, adding, "I was letting go of my own 'rightness.'"

Before long Max faced another crisis. "I realized I'm a catalyst to help people with their communication; people were searching me out. I knew I wanted to change how business is done," he explained. "I wanted to assist in helping people find the gifts and talents they inherently, and usually unconsciously, carry. To do my dream, however, meant transforming my company first."

Naturally, these changes affected his relationship with his business partner. His partner wanted to buy out Max, but he said no. Max then attempted to bring some other senior employees into a multiple-partnership arrangement that would provide a means to buy out his original partner. This deal was going smoothly at first but started to unravel at the eleventh hour when his partners-to-be said, "There is something we see in you—something that you do not trust in us." Max saw that his position in the transactions had reflected his old self: "I know what is right" was just a step away from "He does not really trust us." Max had not realized how great an issue trust continued to be in his life. Trust with people came easily to him at first, but then he could not sustain it and go deeper with it. The prospective partners had seen this. Max said it all came down to giving up control and not having to be right. Yet he still did not know what letting go really meant.

Three months later, Max gave the group what they asked for—more shares at a lower cost. The group of four bought all the shares from the original senior partner who had wanted out. Eventually one new partner left, but the rest remained. Max now had 58 percent of the ownership, and the other three each owned approximately 14 percent.

For a long time, they moved forward successfully. Within five years, the firm had grown into an international company from the development of this new core with several hundred employees in twelve countries. In recognition of the achievement of their aggressive goals, the new partnership had taken the employees and their spouses to the Bahamas for an all-company meeting. Another year passed, and Max thought they were truly a team—until one day when the other partners said, "If we are really going to transform our company and not just change it, then let's really share—if we are going to be what we say." One partner said clearly, "We're not following you because of your shares or the money, but because of who you are." Another said, "If you want to do this, you have to give up control." Max was stunned—both by their statements about the imbalance of the shares and by the idea of giving up control. He truly thought he *had* given up control.

Max thought hard and asked himself, "Here it is; it's really in front of me. What would I have to do to give up control? What would it take to do this?" These questions haunted him at night. When the decision meeting came, Max opened up about his past and told stories of childhood fears, of his mother leaving him so she could be hospitalized for a month when he was two and of his doubts about his brothers' acceptance of him. The group, hearing this, thought Max was going to say no. Instead, Max said yes, and immediately he felt the mantle of responsibility fall away. He re-called that at that point the weight became balanced among them all. He realized, "Here are the people who are doing it. . . . You build real, deep trust when you expose your vulnerability, and those you trust do not use it to hurt you. It is the same in life as in business. We are now equal partners."

Max's trust continued to deepen. When he was celebrating his fiftieth birthday with his partners on a fishing trip, he said at the celebration dinner, "You three are the ones I trust most with my future." Today, Max knows that his phantom fears from the past, his shadows, are still with him, but with vigilance they no longer visit regularly.

Max has a purpose and believes in his people, knowing that they can indeed become leaders in changing how business is done when he gives them the opportunity to truly be who they are, to find their gifts, and to do what they are uniquely able to do as a result. The group members were committed to build a company that performs in all aspects to lead this corporate change around the world. Their philosophy is even reflected in how they bring new people on board. In the beginning, they enticed new employees by telling them they would get rich doing this work. Today they are offering a wellness environment, focusing on being healthy in every aspect of their lives—family, personal health, money, profession, and spirituality. This new vision is reflected in the company's roster. It lists all employees' spouses, partners, and children, and their birth dates. Max now works a four-day week and takes time for his wife and children. The company sponsors Special Olympics and cancer foundations, as well as the community volunteer efforts of current and former employees.

Max's actions demonstrate the movement from personal change to corporate transformation. His transformation required a spiritual leap. His change process took him through the processes of letting go, giving up control, and willingly allowing spirit in his life—which led to corporate transformation. He truly has an ignited spirit today, leading the way for others.

Providing Context for "the Invisible"

René Daumal, author of *Mt. Analogue: A Novel of Symbolically Authentic Non-Euclidian Adventures in Mountain Climbing*,[5] has said, "The door to the invisible must be visible." Who would have thought that corporations could provide the context for meeting "the invisible"? In recent years, we have seen an increase of spiritual practices, such as mindfulness meditation, the Twelve Steps, and brown-bag values discussion groups, in the workplace. Many cities have local organizations in which leaders gather together to share their stories, share their vulnerabilities, and speak in a language often unheard in the workplace.

One example of using spiritual principles that I found to be profound occurred in a client's high-tech firm on the West Coast. He invited me to join a Monday morning meeting, where the senior-management team all sat in relaxed clothing and relaxed positions. They had no agenda; they were there to discover what was in their circle that morning. There may be profound statements; there could be long stretches of silence. There appeared to be no competition. Ideas came forth, without a pattern. This, they told me, is part of their weekly ritual, one hour set aside each week to "be" in their in-novative process.

Despite the openness to personal and spiritual growth in many com-panies, the air still holds a whiff of a cynical attitude many people cling to that most corporations are dishonest, corrupt, and greedy. To the extent that this is true, I hope I've made a case that people in most corporations want to do the right work for the right reasons. And as I hope this book shows, this is more likely to occur when leaders at all levels focus on their personal development and explore their past to discover what shaped them.

It has been a privilege and a delight to witness so many leaders' awakenings—all because they had the courage to "go home." We all know that some cynical, profit-driven, narcissistic leaders will not choose to do this work; it may be too frightening for them to face their vulnerabilities, their shadows, their soft sides. But I do believe that most of these people operate out of unintentional denial and fear. Since they are not in touch with their true values, they choose to sacrifice their integrity in an attempt to play out the cultural myths of what it takes to belong and to succeed. They are often seduced into models of power and domination.

I recall my family mentor saying that we are all family fragments. And as fragments we can recognize that our first family gave us our compass for setting our directions in life. As we know, some were given highly functional compasses; others were given compasses with broken needles. But our compasses do not have to determine our future: we can indeed find a true course when we look inside and find where repairs are needed.

With damaged compasses, or in some cases no compass at all, it is easy to see how shame-bound people in particular can adopt fraudulent selves, facades of power and control as a way to succeed, imitating the image-makers who show well, who speak well. What they later learn when they face their own stories and their own vul-nerabilities is that they were so shut down emotionally that their intuition had stopped functioning—and as philosopher Suzanne Langer has said, intuition is "the highest form of knowing."

For many years I worked with whole families in therapy, and when I began to work with individuals, I realized that I had to work with each person's "family inside"—the first organization where they learned their roles and behaviors. Similarly, in my work with corporate clients, I found it as important for them to make the connection between their own family systems and the systems they created in the workplace. Working with these families, individuals, and companies led me down a long path of learning. I still consider it a privilege to have heard the stories that clients had the courage to reveal when they were willing to step into their pasts and into their shadows. By having the courage to explore their pasts and then revealing their truths, they have given those of us in the consulting field immense data for advancing human development and for creating models that can truly advance ethics and integrity at work.

My vision is that when more leaders offer opportunities for growth and model "genuine leadership," we can then see greater systemic change—in company cultures, in personal family systems, and in our communities. Decisions made in the boardroom affect entire cities and communities. For many years, a strong disconnect has existed between the relationship of our work world and our community lives. In addition to bringing jobs and wealth to communities, companies can take their responsibility seriously in how they can help shape a community for the good.

The workplace has become a source of personal development for millions of people—and what better place for change and transformation! The result is truly a win-win. The owners or senior management win by becoming trusted leaders, the employees win by recognizing their skills are respected, and their families win because these skills and the respect are most often carried home. Eventually the focus of personal development in seats of power in the workplace trickles down into our communities.

While this book focuses on our world of work, it is important to recognize how many ways we lead. How are we leading in our families, our community organizations, our religious institutions? When we can focus on becoming genuine leaders, we can transfer our authenticity to all aspects of our lives. There is indeed a horizon of hope when we can focus on some of the success stories of the genuine leaders who do care, who do want to see ethical best practices in their workplaces and in their communities. When we focus on our own integrity, authenticity, and personal growth, we can not only change the work environment but also we can move our society forward to become a genuine leader in the world.

Pathways for Change

The following exercise is a useful tool for you to continue to explore the ideas from this chapter.

Developing a Spiritual Growth Plan

1. Start with writing your spiritual autobiography. This often includes the influence of religious teachings, personal teachers, and life experiences where you have experienced what you would call "spirituality."

2. Learn to breathe correctly. Mary Alice Winchell, in *One Breath at a Time*, teaches ten guided breath patterns on her CD and DVD (Inner Systems, 2005).

3. Practice stillness. Allow yourself to have 15 minutes a day to meditate. If you choose not to meditate, just sit in a comfortable place and close your eyes, keep your hands in your lap and your feet on the floor, and see what comes.

4. Read. Some good choices are day-at-a-time books, including the following:

   Karen Casey, *Each Day a New Beginning: Daily Meditations for Women* (Center City, MN: Hazelden, 1996).

   Marilyn Mason, *Igniting the Spirit at Work* (Center City, MN: Hazelden, 2001).

   Courage to Change: One Day at a Time in Al-Anon (New York: Al-Anon Family Groups, 1992).

5. Keep a journal. Learn what's going on inside! Include daily affirmations in your journal beginning with "I deserve . . ." Write each affirmation ten times, twice a day if possible.

6. Find online guided imagery exercises.

Notes

Acknowledgments

1. Ivan Boszomenyi-Nagy and Geraldine Sparks, *Invisible Loyalties: Reciprocity in Intergenerational Family Therapy* (London: Routledge, 1973).

Introduction

1. Daniel J. Siegel, *Mindsight: The New Science of Personal Transformation* (New York: Bantam, 2010); quote from presentation in Santa Fe, New Mexico.

2. Ed Michaels, Helen Handfield-Jones, and Beth Axelrod, *The War for Talent* (Boston: Harvard Business Review Press, 2001).

3. Malcolm Gladwell, "The Talent Myth," *The New Yorker,* July 22, 2002.

4. Bill George, *True North: Discover Your Authentic Leadership,* with Peter Sims (San Francisco: Jossey-Bass, 2007).

5. Ernest Becker, *The Birth and Death of Meaning: An Interdisciplinary Perspective on the Problem of Man,* 2nd ed. (New York: The Free Press, 1971), 149.

6. Stephanie Brown, *Treating Adult Children of Alcoholics: A Developmental Perspective* (Hoboken, NJ: John Wiley & Sons, 1989), 43.

7. "The High Cost of Disengaged Employees," *Gallup Business Journal,* April 15, 2002.

8. Alan E. Hall, "Bosses: What Will You Do Differently Today?" *HBR Blog Network,* October 26, 2012.

9. E. E. Bouchery, H. J. Harwood, J. J. Sacks, C. J. Simon, and R. D. Brewer, "Economic Costs of Excessive Alcohol Consumption in the U.S., 2006," *American Journal of Preventive Medicine* 41 (2011): 516–524, quoted in CADCA's National Coalition Institute, "The Economic Costs of Excessive Alcohol Consumption," *Research into Action* (Jan./Feb. 2012), http://www.cadca.org/resources/detail/economic-costs-excessive-alcohol-consumption.

10. "Gallup Study: Unhappy Workers Are Unhealthy Too," *Gallup Business Journal* January 13, 2005, http://businessjournal.gallup.com/content/14545/gallup-study-unhappy-workers-unhealthy-too.aspx.

11. Susan Combs, "Window on State Government," February 2011.

12. Mike Robbins, *Focus on the Good Stuff: The Power of Appreciation* (San Francisco: Jossey-Bass, 2007), quoted in Matthew Kirdahy, "Why Is It So Hard To Say 'Well Done'?" *Forbes,* September 13, 2007, http://www.forbes.com/2007/09/13/workplace-careers-recognition-lead-careers-cx_mk_0913robbins.html.

13. Leadership IQ, "About Our Research," http://www.leadershipiq.com/research -insights/about-our-research/.

14. Stacy Nathan, "Why Do Newly Hired Executives Fail Within 18 Months?" Personalysis Corporation, https://www.personalysis.com/About_Us/Press_Room /Articles/Why_Do_Newly_Hired_Executives_Fail_Within_18_Months/; Staffing Advisor, "Heidrick & Struggles Discovers Its Failure Rate," *Fulcrum Transitions,* 2010, http://www.fulcrumtransitions.com/ricks-and-costs-of-failure/.

15. Stacy Nathan, "Why Do Newly Hired Executives Fail Within 18 Months?" Personalysis Corporation, https://www.personalysis.com/About_Us/Press_Room /Articles/Why_Do_Newly_Hired_Executives_Fail_Within_18_Months/.

16. Brené Brown, *Daring Greatly: How the Courage to Be Vulnerable Transforms the Way We Live, Love, Parent, and Lead* (New York: Gotham, 2012).

Chapter 1: You Can and Should Go Home Again: Finding You

1. National Council on Alcoholism and Drug Dependence, "Learn About Alcohol: FAQs/Facts," http://www.ncadd.org/index.php/learn-about-alcohol/faqsfacts.

2. Lisa Torras, "Preventing Workplace Substance Abuse," *BtoB Guide 2008–2009.*

Chapter 2: Facing Shame and Denial about the Past: Setting Boundaries in the Present

1. Merle Fossum and Marilyn J. Mason, *Facing Shame: Families in Recovery* (New York: W. W. Norton, 1989).

2. Jean-Paul Sartre, *Being and Nothingness* (New York: Citadel Press/Kensington Publishing Corp, 2001).

3. Arthur Miller, *After the Fall,* e-book (New York: Penguin, 2011).

4. Daniel J. Siegel, *The Developing Mind* (New York: Guilford Press, 1999).

5. Bill George, Andrew McLean, and Nick Craig, *Finding Your True North: A Personal Guide* (San Francisco: Jossey-Bass, 2008).

6. Merle Fossum and Marilyn J. Mason, *Facing Shame: Families in Recovery* (New York: W. W. Norton, 1989).

7. Brené Brown, quoted in Drake Baer, "Why Doing Awesome Work Means Making Yourself Vulnerable," *Fast Company,* September 17, 2012, http://www.fastcompany .com/3001319/why-doing-awesome-work-means-making-yourself-vulnerable.

Chapter 3: Leading Change: Leadership Styles

1. Leadership IQ, "About Our Research," http://www.leadershipiq.com /research-insights/about-our-research/.

2. Robert Goffee and Gareth Jones, "Why Should Anyone Be Led by You?" *Harvard Business Review,* September 2000, http://hbr.org/2000/09 /why-should-anyone-be-led-by-you/ar/1.

3. Warren Bennis, *On Becoming a Leader* (New York: Basic Books, 2009).

4. Daniel Goleman, *Primal Leadership* (Boston: Harvard Business School Press, 2002).

5. Jim Collins and Morten Hansen, *Great by Choice: Uncertainty, Chaos, and Luck— Why Some Thrive Despite Them All* (New York: HarperBusiness, 2011).

6. Francesca Di Meglio, "A Crooked Path through B-School?" *Bloomberg Businessweek,* September 23, 2006, http://www.businessweek.com/stories/2006-09-23/a-crooked -path-through-b-school.

7. Noel Tichy, quoted in Arina Isaacson, "Storytelling for Leadership Coaching," Communications Coaching and Consulting site, March 10, 2011, http:// coaching forcommunicationsanfrancisco.com/pages/storytelling-importance.html.

8. Harry Levinson, telephone consultation, May 2002.

9. Michael Maccoby, "Narcissistic Leaders: The Incredible Pros, the Inevitable Cons," *Harvard Business Review,* 2000, revised January 2004, http://hbr.org/2004/01 /narcissistic-leaders-the-incredible-pros-the-inevitable-cons/ar/1.

10. Leigh Buchanan, "13 Ways of Looking at a Leader," *Inc. Magazine,* June 2012, http://www.inc.com/magazine/201206/leigh-buchanan/management-13-ways -of-looking-at-a-leader.html.

11. David Whyte, *The Heart Aroused: Poetry and the Preservation of the Soul in Corporate America* (New York: Doubleday, 1994).

12. Study discussed in Susan Cain, *Quiet: The Power of Introverts in a World That Can't Stop Talking* (New York: Broadway, 2012).

13. Susan Cain, *Quiet: The Power of Introverts in a World That Can't Stop Talking* (New York: Broadway, 2012).

14. Susan Cain, *Quiet: The Power of Introverts in a World That Can't Stop Talking* (New York: Broadway, 2012), quoted in "Leaders Who Don't Build Their Egos," *Matthew Porter Leadership Blog,* June 1, 2013, http://nleaders.wordpress .com/2013/06/01/leaders-who-dont-build-their-egos/.

15. Jim Collins, *Good to Great: Why Some Companies Make the Leap . . . and Others Don't* (New York: HarperCollins Publishers, 2001), 27.

16. John C. Maxwell, *The Difference Maker: Making Your Attitude Your Greatest Asset* (Nashville: Thomas Nelson, 2006), 18.

17. Leadership IQ, "About Our Research," http://www.leadershipiq.com /research-insights/about-our-research/.

18. Leadership IQ study quoted in Mark Murphy, *Hiring for Attitude: Research and Tools to Skyrocket Your Success Rate* (Washington, DC: Leadership IQ, 2012), http://www.leadershipiq.com/materials/Hiring_For_Attitude_1.pdf.

19. Leadership IQ study quoted in Mark Murphy, *Hiring for Attitude: Research and Tools to Skyrocket Your Success Rate* (Washington, DC: Leadership IQ, 2012), http://www.leadershipiq.com/materials/Hiring_For_Attitude_1.pdf.

20. Martin Seligman, *Learned Optimism: How to Change Your Mind and Your Life* (New York: A. A. Knopf, 1991).

21. Queendom.com, quoted in "Do Women Talk More Than Men? Recent Research," Listening Impact blog, December 7, 2011, http://www.listeningimpact .com/2011/12/.

22. Gary Cohen, *Just Ask Leadership: Why Great Managers* Always *Ask the Right Questions* (New York: McGraw-Hill, 2009).

23. Daniel Goleman, "What Makes a Leader?" *Harvard Business Review,* originally published 1998, reprinted January 2004, http://hbr.org/2004/01/what-makes-a-leader.

24. Daniel Goleman, "What Makes a Leader?" *Harvard Business Review,* originally published 1998, reprinted January 2004, http://hbr.org/2004/01/what-makes-a-leader.

25. "EQ and Leadership: Daniel Goleman and Joshua Freedman," YouTube, September 10, 2011, http://www.youtube.com/watch?v=kIQll8F5Xws.

26. Daniel Goleman, *Leadership: The Power of Emotional Intelligence* (Florence, MA: More Than Sound, 2011).

27. Bruce Clarke, "Employees in Teams Suffer without Clear Manager," The View from HR column, January 1, 2012, http://www.newsobserver.com/2012/01/01/1743478/employees-in-teams-suffer-without.html.

28. Persis Swift, "4 Tips to Improve Your Emotional Intelligence in the Workplace," *Workplace Insights,* April 26, 2012, http://blog.capital.org/4-tips-to-improve-your-emotional-intelligence-in-the-workplace/.

29. Martin Seligman, *Learned Optimism: How to Change Your Mind and Your Life* (New York: A. A. Knopf, 1991).

Chapter 4: In a Different Voice: Women Leading

1. Catalyst, "Women CEOs of the Fortune 1000," http://www.catalyst.org/knowledge/women-ceos-fortune-1000.

2. Catalyst, "Women CEOs of the Fortune 1000," http://www.catalyst.org/knowledge/women-ceos-fortune-1000.

3. Caroline Howard, "The New Class Of Female CEOs," *Forbes,* August 22, 2012, http://www.forbes.com/sites/carolinehoward/2012/08/22/introducing-the-new-class-of-female-ceos/.

4. Laura Petrecca, "Number of Female 'Fortune' 500 CEOs at Record High," *USA Today,* October 26, 2011, http://usatoday30.usatoday.com/money/companies/management/story/2011-10-26/women-ceos-fortune-500-companies/50933224/1, quoted in Lyneka Little, "Record Number of Fortune 500 Women CEOs," ABC News, October 27, 2011, http://abcnews.go.com/blogs/business/2011/10/record-number-of-fortune-500-women-ceos/.

5. "The 2013 State of Women-Owned Businesses Report: A Summary of Important Trends 1997-2013," commissioned by American Express OPEN, March 2013, http://www.womenable.com/userfiles/downloads/2013_State_of_Women-Owned_Businesses_Report_FINAL.pdf.

6. Andrew Sherrill, "Women in Management: Female Managers' Representation, Characteristics, and Pay," United States Government Accountability Office, September 28, 2010, http://www.gao.gov/products/GAO-10-1064T.

7. Sheryl Sandberg, *Lean In* (New York: Knopf, 2013).

8. Caliper Corporation, "The Qualities That Distinguish Women Leaders," February 2013, https://www.calipercorp.com/portfolio/the-qualities-that-distinguish -women-leaders/.

9. Barbara B. Moran, "Gender Differences in Leadership," *Library Trends* 40, no. 3 (Winter 1992): 475–91.

10. Catalyst Inc., "Women 'Take Care,' Men 'Take Charge': Stereotyping of U.S. Business Leaders Exposed," Business report, 2005, www.catalyst.org/knowledge /women-take-care-men-take-charge-stereotyping-us-business-leaders-exposed.

11. Sheryl Sandberg, "Why We Have Too Few Women Leaders," TEDWomen talk, Washington, DC, December 21, 2010, 14:58, http://blog.ted.com/2010/12/21 /why-we-have-too-few-women-leaders-sheryl-sandberg-on-ted-com/.

12. "Spa Founder Focuses on Wellness, Philanthropy," *San Diego Union-Tribune,* February 27, 2012, http://www.utsandiego.com/news/2012/Feb/27/spa-founder -focuses-wellness-philanthropy/2/?#article-copy.

13. Bureau of Labor Statistics, "Labor Force Statistics from the Current Population Survey: Wives Who Earn More Than Their Husbands, 1987–2011," last modified November 20, 2012, http://www.bls.gov/cps/wives_earn_more.htm.

14. Kathleen Blanchard, "Trouble with Erections? It Might Be Because Your Wife Earns More Money," February 9, 2013; Emma Gray, "Let's Stop Shaming Women For Outearning Their Male Partners," HuffPost Women blog, February 8, 2013, http://www.huffingtonpost.com/emma-gray/female-breadwinners-husbands -erectile-dysfunction-study_b_2639286.html.

15. Emma Gray, "Let's Stop Shaming Women For Outearning Their Male Partners," HuffPost Women blog, February 8, 2013, http://www.huffingtonpost.com/emma -gray/female-breadwinners-husbands-erectile-dysfunction-study_b_2639286 .html; Catherine New, "Income Gap Closing: Women On Pace To Outearn Men," *Huffington Post,* March 21, 2012, http://www.huffingtonpost.com/2012/03/21 /income-gap-women-make-more-men_n_1368328.html.

16. Belinda Luscombe, "Workplace Salaries: At Last, Women on Top," *Time,* September 1, 2010, http://www.time.com/time/business/article/0,8599,2015274,00.html.

17. Pew Research Center, "The Decline of Marriage And Rise of New Families," November 18, 2010, http://www.pewsocialtrends.org/files/2010/11/pew-social -trends-2010-families.pdf.

18. Pew Research Center, "Fewer Mothers Prefer Full-time Work: From 1997 to 2007," July 12, 2007, http://www.pewsocialtrends.org/2007/07/12/fewer-mothers-prefer -full-time-work/.

19. Child Trends analysis of National Vital Statistics data, quoted in Jason DeParle and Sabrina Tavernise, "For Women Under 30, Most Births Occur Outside Marriage," *New York Times,* February 17, 2012, http://www.nytimes.com/2012/02/18/us /for-women-under-30-most-births-occur-outside-marriage.html?pagewanted =all&_r=0.

20. Alice H. Eagly, Mary C. Johannesen-Schmidt, and Marloes L. van Engen, "Trans-formational, Transactional, and Laissez-Faire Leadership Styles: A Meta-Analysis Comparing Women and Men," *Psychology Bulletin* 129, no. 4 (July 2003): 569–91.

21. Printed with permission from Many Rivers Press, www.davidwhyte.com. David Whyte, "The Journey" in *The House of Belonging,* © Many Rivers Press, Langley, Washington.

22. Catalyst, "2012 Catalyst Census: Fortune 500," December 11, 2012, http://www .catalyst.org/knowledge/2012-catalyst-census-fortune-500.

23. Susan Adams, "10 Things Sheryl Sandberg Gets Exactly Right In 'Lean In,'" *Forbes,* March 4, 2013, http://www.forbes.com/sites/susanadams/2013/03/04/10-things -sheryl-sandberg-gets-exactly-right-in-lean-in/.

24. Spencer Stuart, "Spencer Stuart US Board Index 2012," November 2012, http://www.spencerstuart.com/research/articles/1621/; E. Thames Fulton, "Getting on a Public Company Board," NACD Directorship, May 23, 2013, http://www.directorship.com/how-to-get-a-seat-on-a-public-company-board/.

25. Peter Henning, "Women Lead the Way in White-Collar Law," *New York Times,* Dealbook column, April 2, 2013, http://dealbook.nytimes.com/2013/04/02 /women-lead-the-way-in-white-collar-law.

26. "Women on Corporate Boards Makes Good Business Sense," April 2009, www.womensmedia.com/lead/87-women-on-corporate-boards-makes-good -business-sense.html.

27. Karuna Kumar, "How to Manage Whistleblowing Inside Your Organisation," June 8, 2012, http://www.simply-communicate.com/news/communication/how -manage-whistleblowing-inside-your-organisation; Daniel Goleman, "Dynamics of Whistle Blowing," YouTube, March 1, 2010, http://www.youtube.com /watch?v=kKP_fTI0AAo.

28. Rachel Hare-Mustin, consultation, November 2003.

29. Lynn Banis, "Challenges for Women in Leadership," Ezine Articles, September 24, 2010, http://ezinearticles.com/?Challenges-for-Women-in-Leadership&id=5090354. Used with permission.

30. Bill George, *True North: Discover Your Authentic Leadership,* with Peter Sims (San Francisco: Jossey-Bass, 2007).

Chapter 5: Finding Your Genuine Leader: Stepping into the Light

1. John D. Mayer, David R. Caruso, and Peter Salovey, "Emotional Intelligence Meets Traditional Standards for an Intelligence," *Intelligence* 27, no. 4 (2000): 267–298.

2. John D. Mayer, David R. Caruso, and Peter Salovey, "Emotional Intelligence Meets Traditional Standards for an Intelligence," *Intelligence* 27, no. 4 (2000): 267–298.

3. Daniel J. Siegel, *Mindsight: The New Science of Personal Transformation* (New York: Bantam, 2010).

4. Bill George, *True North: Discover Your Authentic Leadership,* with Peter Sims (San Francisco: Jossey-Bass, 2007); Bill George, *Authentic Leadership: Rediscovering the Secrets to Creating Lasting Value* (San Francisco: Jossey-Bass, 2004).

5. Bill George, personal interview, 2011.

6. Kahlil Gibran, *The Prophet* (Eastford, CT: Martino Publishing, 2011, original 1926).

7. Imagemakers International, "Leadership Training: What Is a Genuine Leader?" Imagemakers International website, 2011, http://www.imagemakersintl.com /leadership-training.html.

8. Boston College Center for Corporate Citizenship and Reputation Institute, "The 2011 CSRI 50," http://www.bcccc.net/pdf/CSRIReport2011.pdf.

9. Boston College Center for Corporate Citizenship and Reputation Institute, "The 2010 Corporate Social Responsibility Index," http://www.bcccc.net/pdf /CSRIReport2010.pdf.

Chapter 6: The Way Through: Company Cultures in Flux

1. Peter Senge, *The Fifth Discipline: The Art and Practice of the Learning Organization* (New York: Currency, 1990).

2. David Wallace, "Infographic: The Most Tried and Failed Small Businesses," *Small Business Trends,* March 25, 2013, http://smallbiztrends.com/2013/03/infographic -failed-small-businesses.html.

3. "Prologue: The Lifespan of a Company," in *The Living Company: Habits for Survival in a Turbulent Business Environment,* posted on *Businessweek,* http://www.businessweek.com/chapter/degeus.htm.

4. John B. McGuire, Charles J. Palus, William Pasmore, and Gary B. Rhodes, *Transforming Your Organization,* Global Organizational Development White Paper Series (Greensboro, NC: Center for Creative Leadership, 2009), http://www .ccl.org/leadership/pdf/solutions/TYO.pdf.

5. Arie de Geus, *The Living Company: Habits for Survival in a Turbulent Business Environment* (New York: Longview Publishing Ltd., 1997).

6. Arie de Geus, *The Living Company: Habits for Survival in a Turbulent Business Environment* (New York: Longview Publishing Ltd., 1997).

7. Marjorie Kelly and William Greider, *The Divine Right of Capital: Dethroning the Corporate Aristocracy* (San Francisco: Berrett-Koehler, 2003).

8. Mike Robbins, *Focus on the Good Stuff: The Power of Appreciation* (San Francisco: Jossey-Bass, 2007), quoted in Matthew Kirdahy, "Why Is It So Hard To Say 'Well Done'?" *Forbes,* September 13, 2007, http://www.forbes.com/2007/09/13/workplace -careers-recognition-lead-careers-cx_mk_0913robbins.html.

9. Warren Buffet, quoted in Sam Mountford, "Why Businesses Suffer from a Trust Gap," GreenBiz.com, April 5, 2012, http://www.greenbiz.com/blog/2012/04/05/ why-businesses-are-suffering-trust-gap.

10. Stephen M. R. Covey, "How the Best Leaders Build Trust," *Leadership Now,* 2009, http://www.leadershipnow.com/CoveyOnTrust.html.

11. Susan Adams, "Trust in CEOs Plummets, But Still Beats Trust in Government," *Forbes,* January 23, 2012, http://www.forbes.com/sites/susanadams/2012/01/23 /trust-in-ceos-plummets-but-still-beats-trust-in-government/.

12. Association of Certified Fraud Examiners, "Report to the Nations on Occupational Fraud and Abuse: 2012 Global Fraud Survey," http://www.acfe.com/uploadedFiles /ACFE_Website/Content/rttn/2012-report-to-nations.pdf.

13. "The High Cost of Low Trust," *Twin Cities Business,* July 1, 2011, http://tcbmag .com/Opinion/Columns/Corner-Office/corner-office-The-High-Cost-of-Low -Trust-July-2011.

14. Stephen M. R. Covey, "How the Best Leaders Build Trust," *Leadership Now,* 2009, http://www.leadershipnow.com/CoveyOnTrust.html.

Chapter 7: When Home Values Are Company Values: Keeping It in the Family

1. PRNewswire, "New Ask.com Study Reveals Workplace Productivity Killers," news release, May 7, 2013, http://www.prnewswire.com/news-releases/new-askcom -study-reveals-workplace-productivity-killers-206398681.html. Research was conducted by Harris Institute on behalf of Ask.com among 2,060 adults ages eighteen and older.

2. Susan Cain, *Quiet: The Power of Introverts in a World That Can't Stop Talking* (New York: Broadway, 2012).

3. Michael K. Allio, "Family Businesses: Their Virtues, Vices, and Strategic Path," *Strategy and Leadership* 32, no. 4 (July/August 2004).

Chapter 8: Leading from Within: Igniting the Spirit at Work

1. Rosabeth Moss Kanter, *The Change Masters: Innovation and Entrepreneurship in the American Corporation* (New York: Simon and Schuster, 1984).

2. "Spiritual Unfoldment Society," *Washington Post,* 1993.

3. Richard Barrett, *Liberating the Corporate Soul: Building a Visionary Organization* (London: Routledge, 2011).

4. Corrine McLaughlin, "Spirituality and Ethics in Business," Center for Visionary Leadership, 2009, http://www.visionarylead.org/articles/spbus.htm.

5. René Daumal, *Mt. Analogue: A Novel of Symbolically Authentic Non-Euclidian Adventures in Mountain Climbing* (New York: Penguin, 1974).

About the Author

Marilyn J. Mason, Ph.D., is an author, speaker, and management consultant. A corporate psychologist and former training director for Rapid Change Technologies, Marilyn specializes in executive leadership development and change management. Marilyn brings her background in communications and family systems into corporate, family foundation, and family business consulting. A former faculty member at the University of Minnesota and a consultant to many corporate groups, Marilyn has coached hundreds of senior executives and CEOs in a variety of businesses, ranging from small to *Fortune* 50 companies.

In addition to leading seminars and retreats, Marilyn lectures nationally and internationally and speaks to radio and TV audiences. She has appeared five times on the *Oprah Winfrey Show.* She is the founding director of Journeys Inward, an adventure travel company in which she leads cross-cultural outdoor wilderness journeys for clients to "meet a culture, meet a group, and meet yourself." She has led treks, climbs, raft trips, and bicycle trips through Tibet, China, Greece, the Caucasus, Peru's Inca Trail, and Africa's Mt. Kilimanjaro and Mt. Meru. She also leads corporate retreats in team-based experiential learning.

Marilyn is the author of *Igniting the Spirit at Work: Making Our Lives Our Own* and *Seven Mountains: Life Lessons from a Climber's Journal* and the coauthor of *Facing Shame: Families in Recovery.*

Marilyn has a Ph.D. in Human Ecology from the University of Minnesota, where she was honored as Outstanding Alumni. Her undergraduate school, Culver Stockton College, chose her as the recipient of its Distinguished Alumni award.

Her work has been recognized in the *New York Times, USA Today, Wall Street Journal, St. Paul Pioneer Press, San Francisco Chronicle, Los Angeles Times,* and CNN Television, and she was featured on *Portraits,* a public television program.

Marilyn has been deeply involved in her communities. She has served on many boards, including Voyageur Outward Bound School, Tibetan American Foundation of Minnesota (chair), Monte del Sol Charter School (board chair), Family Therapy Academy, International Women's Forum (past president), Women's International Study Center (founding member), Rancho La Puerta Board of Directors, Georgia O'Keeffe Women of Distinction committee (founding chair), Museum of New Mexico Foundation, and Hazelden Foundation. She is board president of KSFR Community Public Radio Station in Santa Fe, New Mexico.